KOREA
REBORN

PRENTICE-HALL, INC., Englewood Cliffs, New Jersey 07632

Park Chung Hee

KOREA REBORN

A Model for Development

Library of Congress Cataloging in Publication Data

Pak, Chong-hui, (date)
  Korea reborn.

  Includes index.
    1. Korea—Politics and government—1960-
I. Title.
DS922.35.P3   320.9′519′043   79-11558
ISBN 0-13-516831-7

Printed in the United States of America

10 9 8 7 6 5 4 3 2 1

PRENTICE-HALL INTERNATIONAL, INC., *London*
PRENTICE-HALL OF AUSTRALIA PTY. LIMITED, *Sydney*
PRENTICE-HALL OF CANADA, LTD., *Toronto*
PRENTICE-HALL OF INDIA PRIVATE LIMITED, *New Delhi*
PRENTICE-HALL OF JAPAN, INC., *Tokyo*
PRENTICE-HALL OF SOUTHEAST ASIA PTE. LTD., *Singapore*
WHITEHALL BOOKS LIMITED, *Wellington, New Zealand*

Contents

Foreword 7

introduction

On the Threshold of a New History 11

chapter 1

In Search of Our Identity 19

The Spirit of JAJU 21
Harmony as a Way of Life 24
The Power of Creativity 29

chapter 2

**The YUSHIN Reforms
and Political Development** 37

Beyond the Politics of Imitation 40
A Productive Political Style 47
Ethics of a Democratic Society 59

chapter 3

**The SAEMAUL Movement
and Nation-Building**   67

Removing the Yoke of Poverty 69
Diligence, Self-help and Cooperation 76
Participation and Practice 82

chapter 4

Toward a New Industrial State   89

Energy for Economic Development 91
Stability, Growth and Welfare 97
Toward a Compassionate Society 105

chapter 5

Korea in the World Community   113

From Peace to Unification 115
Stability and Change in International Order 126
An Era of Active Contribution 135

conclusion

Korea's Path to Regeneration   141

Index   147

Foreword

Economic development and modernization have been the single most important theme of the Korean government over the last decade or so. This book is the result of random observations recorded and notes taken in the course of promoting that policy.

Since the launching of the *Saemaul* (New Community) movement, I have been almost totally preoccupied with the question of how better to change our tradition-bound farming communities. As this involves the task of introducing a new spiritual attitude, the *Saemaul* movement is an important part of our country's nation-building program.

Reflecting on our historical legacy and discussing the need for underscoring the uniqueness of Korea's own cultural and political traditions, this book was originally conceived primarily for Korean readers. Some, however, have argued that the experiences that we gained in the course of modernization and economic development might have some relevance to other developing countries, with problems and historical legacies similar to ours, and so suggested that an English-language edition be brought forth. This is why this edition was published.

The editors have kindly added a series of footnotes to make my references to Korea's historical events and personalities easier for foreigners to comprehend. I thank them for this painstaking effort. If this book leads to a better under-standing of Korea's problems and how we propose to attack and solve them, it will have served its modest purpose.

PARK CHUNG HEE
June, 1979
Seoul, Korea

KOREA
REBORN

Introduction:
On the Threshold of a New History

Introduction

As I survey the footprints left by preceding generations and fix my gaze beyond on the future of our posterity, I am moved to feel that ours is a generation that is passing through a truly momentous phase in our nation's long history.

As a reward for our hard work and dedication, the decade of 1970 has been turned into one of the most significant in the annals of Korea. By overcoming such trials and tribulations as perhaps no other people have gone through, the Korean people now proudly step in line to join the rank of nations around the world. Not only have we awakened ourselves from long lethargy and stagnation to knock on the doors of a new historical era; we have begun to tap our national potential hidden in the eternity of five thousand years of recorded history.

Vivid changes and developments are everywhere. The poverty and aimlessness that marked our life at one time have been replaced by a new confidence and determination to bring about an affluent society. In the place of instability and disorder, a foundation for stability and order is being laid out. Having rid ourselves of our history's legacy of subservience to bigger nations and cast away our age-old temptation to depend on others, the Korean people have become vibrant in the new spirit of *jaju*—political independence—and economic self-reliance.

Faces of our average citizens today shine with vitality

and determination; wherever one travels around the world nowadays, one cannot miss feeling the pulse of a new Korea and of new Koreans. At no time in Korea's recent history has the image of our people been so proud and bright. As I reflect on the past thirty years of our generation which walked over a path so strewn with thorns, I cannot but be moved at the shining contrast that today presents.

The post–1945 history of Korea had been unusually turbulent and harsh, so much so that our future at one time seemed only cloudy and hopeless. The joy of emancipation from Japan's colonial rule was swiftly dissipated by the shock of a brutal dismemberment of our national territory. Hopes and the expectation of building a prosperous nation disappeared in the smoke of a fratricidal war.

From the depth of disorder and confusion brought on by our thoughtless imitation of a foreign political system, the pattern of our life continued in a never ending circle of poverty and instability. Fortunately, however, these tribulations and hardships have not been in vain. From the depth of such sufferings sprang forth a new determination and hope. The more painful our wounds of war and territorial division, the fiercer became our craving for peace and unity. Often unbearable was our life of poverty and commotion; but our determination to bring about affluence and stability only became firmer. Even in the darkest hour of our nation's history, each one of us, clenching our fists to collect new energy, began to determine that we must stand up.

This national awareness in the 1960s led to the beginning of the modernization of our country. To reawaken our people's consciousness from its long slumber was never easy. Even harder was the task of reconstructing our nation with our bare hands. After so many twists and turns, the determination to develop was ultimately fired, bringing waves of modernization to our nation's politics, economy, society and culture.

Such awareness and the resulting accomplishments of the 1960s eventually formed the basis of *Yushin*[1] (Revitalizing) Reforms, which caused great spiritual and institutional changes in the 1970s. The Reforms enabled us to react actively to the changing international environment so that we could insure our survival and preserve our affluence. It now provides us with a new launching pad from which we can leap forward to the goals of regenerating our country and once again unifying Korea.

Just as in a man's life, a nation's also faces watershed moments in history; just as a man's life can change in a flash, people who occupy a special place in world history can be decisively shaped by events. Because a man's life is finite, but the life of a nation infinite, an historical moment that promises glory is so much more precious. It is in such an epochal moment in history that we find ourselves today.

In the long course of five thousand years of our country's history, how many such chances have we had to regenerate our nation? Certainly, many hearts will be vexed by this question. So weighed down by the force of negative historical conditions have we been that seldom have our people had a chance to stand up and straighten their backs. Condemned to live in a small land crowded by so many people, unendowed by natural resources, past generations endured everlasting poverty without so much as even questioning it. With the peasants eking out a precarious existence from patches of land handed down by their ancestors, they could save almost nothing to improve their pitiful lots.

Making our life more miserable were our bigger neighbors, who seldom gave us peace. Whenever a new power rose on the continent to the north, or from the ocean to the south, Korea was invariably fixed as their first target of aggression, causing us unspeakable hardship. Their repeated in-

[1]In Korean, *Yushin* means revitalizing, reforming, restoring or renovating. The *Yushin* Reforms, which were launched on October 17, 1972, are also known as *Yushin*, *Yushin* Reforms, Revitalizing Reforms, October Revitalizing Reforms and October *Yushin* Reforms.

cursions destroyed our land, life and property. Sometimes for long, sometimes for only short periods, our country fell under their occupation.

Our forefathers survived all these vicissitudes and managed to bequeath to us an ancient history rich in tradition. Indeed, we can now take just pride in our nation's tenacious potential for survival, and in its inexhaustible source of vitality. Whenever such potential was fully realized, our nation invariably stood at a watershed.

If we consider the unification of Korea in the tenth century by the Kingdom of *Silla*[2] an historical turning point, then the reign of King *Sejong*[3] under the *Yi* Dynasty, during which Korean civilization flourished, should be thought of as the time when our nation was greatly regenerated. Thus, at last, for the first time in hundreds of years, our generation has the opportunity to brush aside the tragic misfortunes in our history, to provide, once again, for our nation's unification and regeneration.

Seen from the perspective of five thousand years of history, the last three decades are but a fleeting moment. In that short span of time, however, much have we perceived, much have we learned and much have we accomplished. Because unbearably painful were our tribulations and hardships, progress achieved at their cost is all the more precious. The most valuable reward we acquired in the fight against all odds

[2]*Silla* was one of the three kingdoms that dominated the Korean peninsula from 57 B.C. Founded in the middle of the fourth century and located at the outset in the present-day eastern part of Kyongsang Province, *Silla*, in alliance with the *Tang* Dynasty of China, later conquered two other rival kingdoms, *Paekche* in 660 and *Koguryo* in 668. *Paekche*, occupying the middle and southwestern part of the peninsula, endured from 18 B.C. to A.D. 660. *Koguryo*, founded in 37 B.C., ruled at its height over the largest territory among the three kingdoms, ranging from the central part of the peninsula up to Manchuria. It was conquered in A.D. 668.

[3]King *Sejong*, the fourth royal head of state of the *Yi* Dynasty who reigned from 1418 to 1450, is known as one of the most enlightened and wisest rulers in history. During his reign Korea achieved outstanding progress in political, socioeconomic and cultural fields, experiencing, in particular, the full blooming of a cultural renaissance with the invention of *Hangul*, the Korean alphabet. The *Yi* Dynasty, the third unified kingdom on the Korean peninsula succeeding the Unified *Silla* and *Koryo* dynasties, lasted from 1392 to 1910.

was a new awareness of our hidden potential as a nation. While surmounting internal problems and external threats, we have managed to tap this potential that has so long sustained our national independence. It is this powerful potential that has been harnessed to the *Yushin* Reforms and the *Saemaul* (New Community) movement.[4] This rediscovered potential is now enabling us to forge a new history. In order to regenerate our nation and reunify it, I see the following three major tasks. First is the need to insure our survival and safety as a nation in the face of an incessant communist threat so as to preserve our national legitimacy. Second is to create an affluent society by completing our modernization on the basis of the strenuous efforts such as we have so far exerted. Third is to create a democratic society on the foundation of our own historic reality and culture and tradition. When these goals have been met, our country, peacefully reunified into one, will make a fitting contribution to the progress of world history.

Not a single one of these tasks is easy to accomplish. Nor could any one of them be given priority over the rest. The complexity of our challenge is underscored by the fact that all three of these objectives must be met at the same time. Indeed, what other country is there in the world which has to confront an aggressor while pushing on with its economic construction and political democratization? No matter how challenging these tasks, our progress will continue. A people who fix their sights on the future are rewarded with hope and confidence. A generation aware of its mission should know only exertion and effort.

The rewards of our dedication in sweat and blood will be the opening of a new era of affluence, peace and unification. We will become a society without scarcity; a nation

---

[4]*Saemaul* can be translated as either new village or new community. However, as the *Saemaul* movement, originally intended to increase farm income and raise the rural standard of living, is presently developing into a nationwide movement to increase industrial production and revive traditional ethical relations between people even in urban areas, the term New Community seems more appropriate for *Saemaul*.

without fear of war; a proud member of the international community capable of helping the less fortunate. We will secure a proud legacy to hand down to our posterity.

For a generation that has known poverty and enslavement, dismemberment of the nation's territory and the scourge of war, achievement of this historical mission should be a worthy endeavor. As we perceive this last chance in our history to make good, our shoulders are heavy under the weight of awareness of this mission. A chance like this should not go unused.

The true significance of a transitional period lies in the ability to discover wisdom for the future in the ancient path of history and to elicit validity from our vision of the future. We can assure ourselves a place in world history if we are aware of our mission and proceed to fulfill it. To do so is our duty. And it is this duty that we are trying to perform.

chapter 1
In Search of
Our Identity

chapter 1

In our world today, each nation is busily seeking to effect its own development and changes in its own situation. But only those countries that do so with a clear self-identity succeed in securing for themselves an affluence and development ahead of others. Because a nation's potential is never quite determined by its material resources or size of its territory, but rather by the spirit and wisdom of its collective life, only those countries that succeed in preserving and developing this spirit improve their chances of development.

In the course of trying to generate energy for Korea's own modernization movement, out of my own concern and passion, I have done what I could to restore the spirit and wisdom that guided our forefathers in history. In order to encourage a better understanding of the past, the government has repaired and restored important cultural relics associated with the lives and works of the great men who helped shape Korea's history.

Not so long ago, it used to be fashionable among some of our intellectuals to study the history and acquire the culture of other nations at the expense of our own, or to study the life and thoughts of foreigners, while neglecting to look at our own heritage. Few things are more unfortunate or shameful than this habit. He who does not comprehend himself will not understand others; he who does not grasp his country's past will never understand the world.

Through a renewed awareness of our own identity,

however, we are on the way to rediscovering our values inherent in our own culture and tradition. By digging out our hidden potential and vitality, we are charting a new, brighter future. By perceiving the currents of our ancient traditions and becoming aware of our values, we Koreans are reviving the wisdom of our forefathers in the present.

The true image of our forefathers that we modern-day Koreans try to recover is that of a politically independent people fearlessly fighting off innumerable foreign invasions; that of a peace loving people trying to live in harmony and cooperation with its fellow men and nations; that of a culturally creative people trying wisely to blend a unique philosophical world by carefully mixing foreign cultures with that of its own. The first step toward regenerating our nation should be to reestablish our national identity.

The Spirit of Jaju

Among the many legacies left behind by our forefathers, the spirit of *jaju* is the most priceless. Succinctly speaking, *jaju* means we should be the master of our own house. It is also a way of saying that we, the Korean people, inhabit this beautiful land and that it is Koreans who shaped an ancient history that goes back over five thousand years. Long a homogeneous people who have shared unusual solidarity through thick and thin, we have developed a strong passion for our collective life and our responsibility to it. *Jaju* rests on the belief that because one is the master of his own house, he cannot remain indifferent to its fortunes; that because we, as Koreans, all share this role, no artificial barrier can be erected between ourselves.

In times of national hardship and tragedy, the spirit of *jaju* always asserted itself to create an atmosphere of cooperation and solidarity; in times of national emergency, it was often elevated to the level of unity for national salvation. In other words, *jaju* nearly always formed the source of a powerful vitality for the nation.

The Korean people, having been zealous and protective of peace from time immemorial, always met the challenges presented by numerous foreign invasions by resolute reaction. The soldiers of the *Koguryo* Kingdom, far outnumbered by enemies from *Shui* and *Tang* China, successfully fought off and repelled the aggressors; after over ten years of tenacious struggles, the small Kingdom of *Silla* finally succeeded in unifying all of Korea by defeating the *Tang* Chinese troops. Indeed, even while the Mongols of the north were trampling China, Asia and many parts of Europe under their feet, *Koryo* was perhaps the only country in the world that for forty years put up such fierce resistance against Mongol occupation.

Through the ages, this spirit of *jaju*, so fiercely defended, was enriched by the *Hwarang* Knights[5] and Buddhism-for-National-Salvation movement.[6] As the nation continued to meet many more tribulations ahead, *jaju* became stronger and even fiercer. When the whole nation was united in the spirit of *jaju*, often beyond the barriers of sex, belief, localism and partisan interests, it turned into an enormous power to deter national crisis. When Japan started the War of *Imjin* Year[7] to invade Korea, the Korean people in the spirit of

[5]*Hwarang* was a sort of military academy during the Kingdom of *Silla*. Consisting of youths, mostly of aristocratic birth, the *Hwarang* Knights trained themselves in both traditional martial skills and in the arts, literature and philosophy, dedicating their lives to the lofty goals of the defense of the country in time of war. In practice, they were the driving force behind *Silla's* successful unification of the peninsula.

[6]Buddhist monks are, in principle, expected to seek solely after heavenly truth, keeping themselves aloof from secular life. But it was in line with the ancient tradition of Korean Buddhism that Buddhist priests courageously rose up in arms in defense of the nation during many national emergencies caused by external invasions. This Buddhist spirit-for-national-salvation materialized not only as the driving force of the patriotism of *Silla's Hwarang* Knights, but also as the spirit behind the effective resistance to the Hideyoshi invasion in the War of *Imjin*, when Buddhists voluntarily formed a militia to fight against the Japanese invaders.

[7]The war broke out in 1592, the year of *Imjin* in the lunar calendar, as Japan's Hideyoshi, in an attempt to divert the attention of local feudal lords who were piling up wealth and power from trade with Western countries, tried to force Korea's *Yi* Dynasty to permit the Japanese forces a free passage for their invasion of China. By dint of the Korean people's arduous defense and resistance in total unity, the Japanese invaders were repelled after the war, lasting almost seven years, had devastated the country.

jaju quickly helped to organize militias to fight a guerrilla war against the invaders; Buddhist monks rose from their monasteries to bear arms for the salvation of the nation. Indeed, it was a time for all Koreans, beyond the differences of sects and personalities, to stand up and offer their lives for the defense of the fatherland.

Under the influence of divisiveness and subservience, when *jaju* lost its luster, the energy of our people was invariably affected, inviting trials and hardships. A good example is the end of *Yi* Dynasty when, for the first time in history, we completely lost our nation to Japan.

By the time the European powers began to hit our shores in the mid-nineteenth century, Koreans did briefly possess the chance to seek the power of *jaju* to react to events. Then, seeds of modernity were just beginning to bud; patriots with foresight were still calling for a policy of "enrich the nation, strengthen its defense," in order to keep pace with the march of time. Unfortunately for our forefathers, however, they lacked the power to produce a centripetal force to organize and unify their efforts behind this policy. As their modernization efforts lagged behind, Korea as a nation, falling a victim of Big Power rivalry, disappeared.

Had the leaders and the led then been firmly united, concentrating their efforts to strengthen the nation's power, the tragedy of Japan's occupation of Korea might have been averted. By failing to perceive the nature of changes in the international situation and indulging themselves in schisms and blatant dependence on foreigners, our leaders at that time could not but leave behind for us a legacy of excruciating sorrow. Korea, as a result of that, was condemned to trail behind in the march of history.

From this experience, we learn the lesson of the heavy responsibility of any generation that finds itself at a turning point in history. That generation, which failed grievously to sustain the nation's independence, soon brought foreign occupation and a subsequent dismemberment of our nation's territory. An individual in need of help could always turn to his family or friends; but a nation in need of *jaju* could hardly expect help from other nations. The price we paid for this was Japan's domination and our enslavery.

It is an irony of history that even in the severest moments of foreign domination, however, the spirit of *jaju* never completely died out. Both at home and abroad, our patriots rallied their forces to fight for emancipation, eventually climaxing in the 1919 March First Independence Movement.[8] Later, as the harsh colonial policy of Japan sought to exterminate our language and ethos, the tradition and spirit of *jaju*, as well as our belief in unity, again rose to preserve our culture until the day of final liberation. Indeed, it was an example of our nation's potential rising from its slumber to meet the level of severity of our hardships and tribulations. What other people in the world can take a pride, as we do, from having successfully preserved our homogeneity under so many foreign aggressions? Many a strong nation and people have disappeared without trace in the course of human history. That we have lasted so far is clearly a surprise and source of pride.

Harmony as a Way of Life

While our zeal for peace is thus rooted in the spirit of *jaju*, Koreans, throughout the ages, have held human relationships based on harmony and moderation in high regard. Originally an agrarian people who began to settle on the peninsula from time immemorial, they were, by disposition, peaceful and fraternal. By blending the northern continental temperaments with southern maritime cultures, we formed a unique spiritual world for ourselves.

[8]Aware of the international trend endorsing the self-determination of nations as declared in U.S. President Woodrow Wilson's Fourteen Points, the Korean people, who had for a decade been under the rule of the Japanese occupation authorities, fired a nationwide independence movement on March 1, 1919, characterized primarily by the goal of achieving national independence based on modern nationalism and by its means of absolute nonviolence even against the oppressors. The Movement is recorded in history as the launching pad for Korea's difficult struggle toward independence, modernization, and peace.

Lying between the continent of China and Sea of Japan, the peninsula's peculiar geography and topography have endowed the Korean people with the toughness and grandiose spirit of the continent, as well as the passion and optimism of the sea. If our tenacious resistance to so many foreign invasions is a reflection of continental traits, then our zeal for peace and our aesthetic values can be attributed to maritime influences. Having shaped a unique mental attitude from these two dominant sources, with the result of belonging neither to the West nor to the East, our people have fashioned a spiritual world of our own with its peculiar rhythm and sense of unity.

Korea's beautiful landscapes and changing seasons have given our people a fine artistic sensibility. Incessant contacts with other cultures have taught us to accept differences without quite being assimilated ourselves. The result was the creation of a unique tradition not only in arts and cultures but also in the whole gamut of lifestyles. We have always displayed a special talent for blending diversities to recreate something new and original. Today's lifestyles are the result of this process being repeated many times over.

We see the essence of this unique way of life and thought as being the spirit of harmony or "hwa." Its characteristic is to regard human or social relationships not on the basis of conflict and struggle, but on the basis of harmony and cooperation. It is an attitude of life and mentality that insists that although conflicts and confrontations often divide man from man, or man from the state, there is always bound to be a common ground that makes complementary relationships and mutual development possible.

The spirit of harmony holds tolerance, justice and reason above confrontation, contradiction, struggle and bickering. Throughout history we have surely shown a preference for harmony over conflicts, peace over violence. The devastation of the many wars that mark the progress of our history is often cited to explain this tendency; in reality, however, its roots are to be found in our people's ingrained mild temperament; their dedication to the harmonious development of their society; and their native disposition in favor of peace and cooperation.

By blending individual life with that of the community, we have always considered maintaining a peaceful order as an ideal. Eventually, this tradition formed the backbone of a life ethics based on love and harmony between man and man and peace and cooperation between nation and nation.

This tradition also harks back to the original ideology of our forefathers, the Philosophy of Beneficial Man.[9] This lofty concept that all men should be treated like brothers, originated from a respect for mankind and for peace. It is the notion of treating all private lives as leading to the betterment of human society; that the management of the state has as its ultimate goal the helping of human society. Regardless of which country we belong to, of how strangely we look to each other, all men are ultimately brothers on this globe. Whereas mythologies of many a national foundation stress violence and struggle, our Philosophy of Beneficial Man should be noted for its inclination toward peace and love for fellow human beings.

It is against such an historic tradition that our respect for man is set. The idea that everyone could achieve harmony transcending differences of personality and opinions reflects the belief that men by nature are basically the same and are born equal. It is by no means a narrow individualism, but a broad attitude of sharing our joy as well as our pain together. Take, for example, our timeheld tradition of going immediately to the aid of neighbors in distress, without quite being invited to do so. It is rooted in Korea's tradition of considering cooperation as a supreme virtue.

[9]*Hong Ik In Gan* in Korean is a concept which is aimed at instilling in both people and government a resolve to do good and to benefit all mankind. Proposed originally as the supreme ideology of the nation's foundation by *Tangun*, who is known as the founder of the Korean nation, it has served as a basic principle of politics and religion throughout Korea's five thousand years of history.

This ancient tradition of respecting our fellow man naturally has led to the creation of a political form based on humanism. From ancient Korea, monarchs always considered the people as forming the essence of the nation. The ultimate relevance of politics was to provide the people with a righteous life, following the Mandate of Heaven. The belief that only a politics devoted to the public weal is worthy of the Mandate of Heaven produced the famed, ancient adage: "The minds of the people are the mind of Heaven." The tendency to think that concepts such as equality and democracy are foreign to Korea, as seem to be entertained by some people, could not be more misleading, for they formed a part of our ancient traditions.

Education through the ages has deepened and further cultivated the spirit of harmony and cooperation. The *Hwarang* Knighthood—whose origin goes back to the Buddhism-for-National-Salvation Movement and Korea's ancient chivalry—provided the youth of the *Silla* Kingdom with a training ground for developing a self-awareness as well as a fearless devotion to the state. They found their inspiration not only in tough military training, but also in the cultivation of a taste for literature and the arts. Wandering across the breadth of their land, they sought out places of beauty to seek inspiration. In the building of harmonious relationships, the *Hwarang* Knights also formed a powerful solidarity. Their prototype of a manly man was a knight who would fearlessly give up his life for the defense of his country, but also show compassion for life in all its forms, a fearless man at once determined to protect the cause and honor of the community, but also a romantic, appreciative of the great nature surrounding him. The spirit that moved a *Hwarang* Knight appeared superficially effeminate, but eventually it was his spirit that moved the Kingdom of *Silla* to conquer the neighboring kingdoms of *Paekche* and *Koguryo* to unify Korea in today's shape.

The spirit that moved the life of the *Hwarang* has manifested itself in our people's deep desire for unity. In the course of fighting off manifold foreign invasions, sharing life and death, we acquired an unusual zeal for our country. With each man sealing his fate with that of the state, a harmonious relationship was formed between the individual and his country. From the earliest time onward, we have learned the lesson that the state is not just a collection of people, nor is a state that which just lords itself over individuals. The two differing concepts, through a fusion of solidarity and mutual love, were shaped into a single identity.

Of late, some people try to dismiss the notion of *ch'unghyo* (loyalty to the country and filial respect for parents) as being archaic remnants from ancient Confucianism. Without such a notion guiding one's life, however, one could hardly be considered sincere to himself. Although there is an element of collectivism in it, the notion of *ch'unghyo* has as its central theme the obligation of individuals. For an individual life to be sincere and for human and social relationships to be possible, it must be a harmonious life within a collective entity.

In ancient times, Korea was known as a land of "ritual and decorum." Virtues then included decorum and credibility, compassion for the young and respect for the aged. To help improve the modern-day family and social milieu, the notion is now being revived. Certainly the notion of *ch'unghyo* fits into modern-day standards of morality and ethics.

In Korea, the notion of *ch'unghyo* has hardly been limited to the confines of a single family. Consider the Korean habit of calling one's parents "our parents" instead of "my parents." This habit is rooted in the tradition of reserving the same diffidence and respect for the parents of others. This has led to the maintenance of human relationships based on harmony and warmth for all. It is, in short, the recovery of man's true nature of goodness to all.

In both home and society, this is how peace and order are being satisfactorily preserved. The guiding spirit that underlies this tradition leads also to patriotism and the unusual passion that our people have for our country. It helps to explain many spontaneous movements in Korea's history to rush to her aid in time of distress.

Ch'unghyo is also a love shown for the collective entity to which one belongs. Just as a home is a small collective body, so the state is a larger community. Our love for one should not differ in intensity to that shown to the other. While *"hyo,"* meaning filial love, is a natural expression of love flowing toward one's parents, *"ch'ung"* should be our devotion to the collective entity called the state. One who does not maintain a wholesome family order cannot be expected to show strong devotion to his state.

Our notion of *ch'unghyo* should have even greater relevance to a society with a high level of civilization. The recent industrialization and urbanization are straining our traditional family and social relationships. Nevertheless, it still holds true that human compassion is essential for any individual or social development. The principle that a happy life depends on a harmonious human relationship can be applied simultaneously to the seemingly contradictory goals of individual as well as social development.

Tradition and modernization, freedom and equality, stability and growth, *jaju* and cooperation . . . they are merely different goals that either the state or an individual seeks to pursue. Harmony can rule over these contradictions, if the state or the individual can find common ground.

The Power of Creativity

Our forefathers have left behind us the shining cultural legacy of *jaju* and harmony, but their creativeness also forms the basis of Korea's political, economic, social, religious and scientific accomplishments. They invented the world's first metallic letter type, built armored ships when the rest of the world was sailing on wood, constructed a rain gauge, and invented a scientific system of writing called *Hangul*. In the field of political institutions, one is reminded of the

"*Hwabaek* System" of the *Silla* Kingdom, which made unanimity of opinion on political subjects possible through a building of consensus. "*Uich'ang*" and "*Hwankok*" were two excellent economic-welfare policies of the *Yi* Dynasty by which grains were collected and stored in peacetime for distribution in time of distress. In the field of scholarship, the *Silhak* School of Confucianism—emphasizing pragmatic learning—greatly contributed to the birth of modern Japan and China. When the spirit of *jaju* soared, the creativeness of the Korean people reached its peak. The stronger the spirit of *jaju* reverberated, the more active became our creative energy. Conversely, the more unique was our culture, the stronger ran our *jaju* spirit.

Some of our country's greatest historical accomplishments were recorded while it was engaged in battles for survival. Take the carving of 80,000 woodblocks recording Buddhist scriptures,[10] or the invention of armored "Turtle" ships.[11] Indeed, our people, desperately determined to rise to challenges from within and without, were endowed with a truly great cultural creativeness.

Such wisdom was greatly inspired by the power of harmony—harmony being the process of blending elements foreign from our own and involving the act of creation itself. We have accepted many foreign cultures but always blended them to produce a unique something of our own. Seldom have we been assimilated into them, nor have we ever imitated. As

[10]Harassed by the Mongol invaders for nearly 150 years to the verge of demise, the *Koryo* Dynasty, Korea's second unified kingdom lasting from 918 to 1392, carved the wooden blocks, numbering 81,258, for the printing of the Buddhist Tripitaka Koreana in a gesture to express the nation's devout faith and patriotism and to pray for Buddha's protection against the Mongols. These wooden printing blocks were completed in 1251 and are today preserved without damage in a big temple in the southern part of the country.

[11]The Turtle ship is the world's first iron-clad warship invented by Admiral Yi Sun Shin, who showed his prominence as a naval commander and a model of a patriotic civil servant at the time of the *Imjin* War caused by Hideyoshi's invasion. These ships made a great contribution to the defeat of the Japanese fleets in naval battles fought under Admiral Yi's command close to the south coast of the peninsula, thus arousing horror among Japanese soldiers.

in the time of the Unification of the Three Kingdoms, or under the reign of King *Sejong* of the *Yi* Dynasty, the flowering of our creative spirit coincided with the enhancement of the nation's power far and wide. When our creativeness withered, so did the fortunes of our nation. An excellent example of this is the Closed Door Policy of the *Yi* Dynasty which blocked the inflow of foreign cultures and thus eventually accelerated its own sad demise.

Our ancestors used to have an excellent adage for this. *"On Ko Ji Shin,"* they said, meaning, "Reviewing the old is learning the new." Involving the whole process of creation, it shows how the Korean people have preserved their knowledge, acquired the new, and out of this process, recreated a unique culture of their own. It is through such efforts that we not only preserve what we already have but also contribute to the development of other cultures. As only a unique culture can make a worthy contribution, the cultivation of our culture means the cultivation of world civilization, and hence the development of humanity.

Each nation, with its own uniqueness created and developed from the soils of world culture, helps to diversify and enrich human civilization. Man's progress is the result of lively contacts and exchanges between different cultures, each goading the other's development. Accordingly, although it is difficult to comprehend the contribution of a single, national culture to the flow of world culture, this comprehension is meaningful for us today and thus is a challenge worthy of our endeavors.

Culture, as a general rule, is hardly confined to arts and letters. It crystallizes all the experiences and wisdom that a nation has gained through its long historical process. It contains that nation's aspirations as well as hopes. This explains why a people with an independent and creative culture usually enjoy independence and creativeness in all other fields. In the final analysis, therefore, the question of how better to solve our problems and how effectively to accomplish the task of regenerating our nation depends, to a large extent, on whether or not we are capable of creating a new culture of an even superior quality.

The development of a new national culture is almost tantamount to the setting up of new pillars to sustain fresh historical values. This would also be a priceless legacy to our posterity. As we live at the crossroad of Eastern and Western cultures, our creative efforts are blessed by favorable opportunity and conditions. In the confused melange of cultures brought in by the East and West, Korea, at one time in history, lost its national identity. Now, as it successfully absorbs their meritorious points, strength from the East as well as from the West must be chosen, consciously moulded as ours, and fully developed.

Our daily life should be the starting point for the launching of a new culture. History, being an accumulation of day to day events, can be a tricky thing. A small difference neglected today, leads into a big gap in the future. It was such small differences which eventually led to the huge gap in scientific developments between the East and West. The East, as it were, has had the penchant for revering the past. With people turning to the past for inspiration, progressive efforts to fashion a future were often frustrated. Eastern man, accepting nature and the social environment in a fatalistic manner, stood powerless before nature or God. Even the fortunes of the state were dependent on the so-called Mandate of Heaven. A passive way of life such as this made challenges to nature almost impossible, discouraging man's progress as well as development.

Western man, trying as always to discover the inner laws at work in nature as well as in human society, has seldom taken nature for granted. It was his philosophy to try to find ways to control nature. I believe that it was this spirit of science and pioneering that led to the foundation of Europe and the United States. Their efforts toward modernization received added impetus from the Protestant Ethic arising out of the Reformation. In the early United States, Puritans discovered God's blessing in hard work and believed in success as a temporal blessing. It was with these elements that they eventually succeeded in opening up the New World. These were the spirits that moved the West, which until the fourteenth century was way behind the East, forward. Its rationalism and pragmatism are the strengths of the Western philosophy that we should absorb.

Not everything Western or modern, however, should be considered good and useful. A blind aping of the West is undesirable, for to do so is to abandon our own creativeness. This is the way to enslavement. Throughout recent history, our contacts with the West were dictated to us by the Western encroachments upon Asia, and owing to such an historical background, many of us were deprived of the spirit of *jaju*. To sustain *jaju*, some of our ancestors tried to resist Western encroachments; others tried to hurry their own preparations for modernization. But the power of Western science was always superior, with the result that the East had to just drift; many Easterners came to despise their own roots.

Korea's contacts with the West were even more distorted than usual as they were sought and made by way of Japan, another Asian country. To make things worse, no sooner was Korea emancipated from Japan's colonial control than it was overwhelmed by an avalanche of Western influences. Either to maintain *jaju* or distinguish what was good from what was bad became almost impossible.

Not a few learned people, misled into thinking that modernization was Westernization, blamed our age-old poverty and historical stagnation on Korea's tradition-bound culture. While the north Korean Communist regime is thus bent on destroying everything that is traditional, our intellectuals have made insufficient efforts to understand our own cultural heritage. Some of them, misguided to equate tradition with premodern archaism, even began to believe that to flout tradition was to modernize.

In the case of Korea, to ape the West should never be the goal of industrialization or modernization. Nor should these goals be led to conflict with our own culture and traditions. The East's merits and strengths should be recognized, elements modern in them should be brought out, chosen and then developed. This is how a modern civilization in Korea can be created. Tradition and modernization are not separate but they form a continuity. Instead of slowing down modernization, some of our traditional thoughts and way of life could even stimulate its pace; depending on how we manage them, they can become a source of strength to guide our future course.

The problems afflicting modern industrial societies of the West are good reasons why we should not consider Westernization or modernization necessarily a panacea for all our ills. Gripped by a confusion of values and chronic social instability, the West is now beginning to talk about dehumanization. It might be brushed aside simply as an inevitable by-product of an industrialized society. To me, however, it seems as if this dehumanization has something to do with the life attitude and way of thinking of Westerners.

Influenced by wholly different historical environments, the Eastern and Western ways of life should be drastically different. Asians, as a general rule, tend to be introspective and spiritual. In contrast, Westerners are striking for their active, individualistic and materialistic value system. Whereas Asians tend to be subjective, emotional and comprehensive in their attitude, Westerners are objective, rational and analytical in mind. Korea's culture and traditions should choose only the strengths and merits from these contrasts.

As Western civilization began to attack our shores, some of our predecessors, feeling the urgency to strengthen our national power, proposed a policy to accept Western civilization to make it serve the Eastern spiritual heritage. Our present attempt to blend the East and West meets this objective. To achieve this goal is no doubt difficult, but the more difficult it is, the stronger should be our spirit of *jaju* and creativeness. *Jaju* should be the standard on which to judge what is needed and what is not. In our attempts to assimilate the strengths of two different cultures our skills at blending and recreating a progressive, future-oriented culture and tradition will be tested. The launching of the modernization movement in the 1960s awakened such an awareness. Guided by this awareness, Korea is now on its way to establish a new identity within the political system, the economy, social life, culture and education.

chapter 2
The YUSHIN Reforms and Political Development

chapter 2

The Republic of Korea today is on its way to establishing a genuinely democratic political system that reflects the Korean historical legacy and tradition, the Korean national spirit and wisdom. A political system being basic to a nation, its healthy restoration is the key to the completion of the task of national regeneration. A nation's peace and security, welfare and prosperity, are achieved only through political stability.

Like many other countries that gained independence following 1945, the Republic of Korea also chose democracy as its form of government. Of the various political systems ever invented by mankind, it is democracy that most successfully blends individual liberty with social order. Its essence as well as its strength lie in the system's aim to maintain social order by way of individual self-discipline and responsibility, of attaining social development through the exercise of individual liberty and creativeness. To adopt democracy as a form of government, therefore, was a wise choice.

And yet, the fact remains that no country in the world has a perfect form of democracy. Korea's own experiment with the system since the founding of the Republic in 1948 would indicate how difficult a system it is. As a result of the failure to acquire its essence, Korea over the last twenty years went through serious political instability and upheavals, eventually provoking two successive revolutions. Our short history of experimentation with democracy was a continuation of aimlessness and errors; wastefulness and inefficiency sapped the nation's strength and frustrated Korea's efforts to modernize itself.

At one time, we tried the American presidential system in the hope of imitating an American style of democracy; at another time, we tried British parliamentary government hoping to ape the example of the United Kingdom. For a long time, not a few Koreans believed that imitation of European forms of government would automatically yield a similar political democracy. The basic cause of our repeated failures with political experimentation was our failure to comprehend how a democratic government should work, or which aspects of democracy best suited our purposes.

In order to shape a genuine democratic government in Korea, it is important to distinguish democracy's ideals from its institutions. Its ideals to bring about individual liberty, equality and happiness are shared by all nations of the world. But it remains for every country to shape its own institutions and styles to achieve these goals. Just as each individual has his own lifestyle and personality, and employs his own distinctive manners to achieve his personal goals, so it is with nations. Each nation, influenced by its distinctive historical conditions, different goals and cultural traditions, adopts its own different methods.

There is no guarantee, therefore, that a political system developed by a certain nation could automatically be applied to other nations with different cultures and traditions. The Western democratic system which we adopted for ourselves has been evolved and developed over a long period of time to solve problems that only a European milieu could pose. If and when such an alien system were automatically transplanted to a different country, it not only could not survive but would even cause bad side-effects. Such a conclusion emerges clearly from the difficulties that many newly emerging countries that adopted Western forms of democracy now encounter.

Beyond the Politics of Imitation

The idea of building a genuine democratic political system relevant to the Republic of Korea should start from our acceptance of the fact that Korean reality and problems and Korean cultural traditions are radically different from those of the West. The point of departure starts right from our political traditions.

I believe that the Western European political system grew out of historical and social relationships based on the concept of conflict and confrontation and the principle of solving these conflicts through negotiation and compromise. In short, it has been in Western democracy's tradition to seek out conflicts and expose them, so that both individuals and groups could, by way of friendly competition and compromise, solve them.

The overall goal of social development and order has been achieved by compromising and balancing the different interests of individuals versus groups, the government versus people, the parliament versus the executive branch, the majority versus the minority. A broad public consensus, which accepts the spirit of rationalism and the rule of law, has also given Western European society its strength to maintain social order and stability. In other words, political conflicts have been resolved within a clearly defined framework.

The Western respect for law and order is certainly worthy of our emulation. Indeed, Europeans have made it part of their life ethics to respect a law or policy once it has been decided upon, regardless of how strongly they disagree with it. Such a tradition is sustained by the people's readiness to accept the principle of settling their differences within the framework of law, and this concept is supported by the citizens' exercise of self-discipline. The concept of the rule of law is based on the spirit of rationalism which determines the life of average Westerners. They have also long ago acquired the idea that a law, to be able to function properly and play its role of maintaining social stability, should command the respect of all people, regardless of who they are; that if individual liberty and happiness are to be maintained, that is the only way.

Unfortunately, however, many Oriental societies, including ours, have failed to develop the philosophy of rationalism or the concept of the rule of law to help us to constructively settle political differences and conflicts. We have been particularly lacking in the exercise of self-restraint and self-discipline that are innate to the concept of liberty. We have often neglected the sense of responsibility and obligation that always accompany the exercise of rights. This is why in the name of democracy, destructive, illegal acts that threaten the very basis of a democratic order are sometimes committed. With almost no public awareness of what a productive competition is, political conflicts in Korea have often turned into extreme forms of struggle; democracy's principle of compromise has often turned into unprincipled bickering by politicians.

Looking back over the history of Korea's constitutional form of government, we discover that political differences between the majority and minority, between the legislative and executive branches, or even among politicians themselves, degenerated into exaggerated struggles, in the end creating political unrest and social instability that threaten the very basis of a democratic order. As a result, not only was the implementation of urgent national policies frequently delayed; our country's efforts to modernize itself were frustrated. Korea's repeated failures to modernize economically and socially made these ills appear even more prominent. This, then, was another distinction that marked Korea's difference from countries of the West.

In other words, the Western political system played the role of stabilizing already achieved social and economic development instead of provoking and guiding that development itself. Politics played the important role of shedding light on social conflicts and frictions and of neatly dissecting each problem, so that through friendly competition and compromise, they could be amicably resolved. Therefore, because in the successful democratic countries of the West people did not expect too much from or place too great demands on politics, and because political conflicts were diversified and tended to balance each other out, extreme confrontations could be avoided.

For all that, even Westerners realize that the transplanting of their system of government requires a certain level of economic and social development. But unlike the West, which modernized itself over a long period of time, most developing countries are impatient to achieve rapid modernization, undergoing as a result of such impatience radical transformations in nearly all spheres of endeavors. Peoples of developing countries also entertain far greater expectations about what the political system can achieve for them. If caught in the vortex of severe social transformation, their attempts to imitate West European democracy can result in extreme political unrest and corruption, leading to greater political instability.

In the case of many developing countries, the historical legacies of colonialism and semicolonialism have caused uneven social and economic development. Giving diversified social groups a chance to ventilate their political demands all at once leads to either violent political upheavals or the monopolization of power by a single group. In the final analysis, the entire effort at modernization may be subverted.

Not surprisingly, many nations that after World War II adopted the European form of democracy now possess neither a democracy nor modernization. With chronic instability and turmoil the order of the day, some countries have turned into outright one-party dictatorships while others have fallen victims to poverty and political unrest.

For any nation to modernize itself, it is essential that it try to distribute resources evenly through a scientifically planned policy. If chronic political unrest or corruption frustrates this attempt, then modernization fails grievously.

Meanwhile, if there is no political stability to facilitate the provision of a more affluent life and modernization for the people, the resulting frustration is bound to worsen political unrest.

Still fresh in our memory are the scenes of post–Liberation political unrest when all sorts of social and political organizations literally mushroomed without any significant base of public support. Continuing the familiar pattern of joining together and splitting up at the whim of irresponsible politicians, these organizations were made the tools of self-seeking politicians who were supposed to serve the interests of the groups they allegedly represented. With professional agitators and tricksters pursuing their personal fortunes in the name of democracy, political activities more and more resembled a marketplace. Under such circumstances, fashioning a long-term modernization plan became impossible.

What is to be even more regretted is the fact that in the course of trying blindly to imitate foreign political institutions and styles, the Korean people were beginning to lose sight of their own positive traditions and customs. Moreover, each election campaign, generating emotional confrontation between region and region, clan and clan, neighbor and friend, tore asunder the peaceful fabric of our village life. Irresponsible politicians issued impossible programs to mislead people into believing that an election could automatically bring forth rehabilitation of regional communities. All these trends, in the end, brought nothing but the encouragement of psychological dependence on the government.

In the final analysis, what Korea needs is a democratic system capable of most effectively achieving modernization, a political system which will accord well with Korean lifestyles, culture and tradition. The unique features of Korea's historic background make such a need especially relevant.

The Republic of Korea, with its territory brutally dismembered and lying under the constant military threat from the north Korean Communist regime, has lived since liberation in 1945, and still does, in a state of war or semi-war. Ignoring such an historical condition in our blind attempt to imitate a foreign political system will lead to a situation threatening our national survival rather than solving our problems, which are not shared by countries with which we try to identify.

Even some Western democracies have tried to flexibly manipulate their institutions and basic rights of citizens in such a way as to help solve their national problems. For example, the chief of state in any country possesses emergency powers to protect democracy in time of danger. It is a fact of history that during the American Civil War, when survival of the United States as a nation was being threatened, President Lincoln assumed vast emergency powers, suspended civil rights of American citizens, and even arrested, without warrant, tens of thousands of people suspected of antistate activities. Had the president, bowing to fierce opposition from the Congress, taken what would have been considered peacetime steps that were insufficient to cope with the country's crisis or to protect democracy, I wonder whether an America as strong and as prosperous as she is today would have been created. Had it not been for his swift and bold resolve and decision, the United States today, instead of being one Union, might have been broken into four or five different republics—in which event, modern history would have been radically altered.

President Roosevelt similarly seized emergency powers during the 1930s to lead the United States from its great recession and bring it victorious from its war against totalitarianism. Mr. Roosevelt not only went down in history as the only president of the United States to serve four terms in office, but also as the only president who wielded such enormous emergency powers. By revising the principle of free enterprise, he enforced strict price controls to fight recession; placed Hawaii under emergency declaration to relocate and intern Japanese-Americans in concentrated settlements; and controlled sensational reports of the war by the American press. Many of these harsh measures of course provoked considerable opposition from the American public, but as more and more realized the seriousness of the crisis and the justifiable grounds for the emergency, they not only accepted them but even endorsed them. Because of their roles in protecting democracy in times of crisis, historians nowadays regard Presidents Lincoln and Roosevelt as being two of the greatest presidents in America's history.

Even in France, which is one of the countries where democracy originated, the serious national crisis of the 1950s, bred by the problem of Algeria's independence, led President Charles de Gaulle to prolong his term in office to seven years and to take broad presidential authority to better manage the national administration and preserve political stability. As a result of these measures, France not only successfully coped with the crisis, but even managed to restore past glory and achieve, in all spheres, a shining development. Thanks to the de Gaulle constitution and considerable political stability resulting from it, France, free from political unrest that has attacked many other Western democracies, today offers a drastic contrast.

These examples show how different historical conditions affect the operation of a democracy. To prevent wastefulness and inefficiency, which are apt to be caused by political conflict and struggle, it is considered natural to unite to save democracy itself. The more serious the nature of the crisis, the more have many Western countries sought to give higher priority to the substance of democracy than to its formality; higher priority to unity and efficiency than to the trappings of competition.

Marked by territorial dismemberment and the state of semi-war, conditions in Korea are far more serious and urgent than the crises that grip the countries of Europe. For Korea to overcome its problems and survive as a nation, it needs an efficient form of a democratic system. At one time in recent history, some people refused to accept this simple logic. Preoccupied by democracy's superficial trappings, these people, underestimating the value of self-restraint and responsibility required for promoting liberty itself, often declared they were protecting democracy while ignoring the aspects of substance and efficiency. Democracy was mistaken for unlimited freedom and disorder.

In an open society like ours, which respects individual freedom and creativity, a certain level of conflict and friction—or even disorder—might be acceptable at times. That is to say that the society in the Republic of Korea is much freer and more humane than the one which exists in north Korea. It is a tribute to democracy's strength that while conflict and friction could be considered wasteful and inefficient in the short term, they could be considered, in the long-term perspective, even progressive and creative.

No matter how free a democracy should be, however, it must have a limit of tolerance, and such a limit cannot but be different in every nation. In a country like the United States, which has no adversary on its borders but a vast military and economic capability to defend itself from outside attack, a certain degree of tolerance for wastefulness and inefficiency will not endanger its survival. Not so for a nation like the Republic of Korea, which shares borders with a hostile regime of communist aggressors. With its defense still relatively weak, its level of tolerance for conflict and struggle, for wastefulness and inefficiency, obviously cannot match those of the United States.

Should our nation, forgetting the obvious limit to tolerance imposed by our country's reality, continue its pattern of fruitless political conflict and struggle, we would unwittingly lay ourselves open to agitation by subversive elements bent upon destroying our nation's foundation. If such a situation were to come to pass, instead of strengthening the nation's power to overcome such problems as territorial dismemberment and the crisis resulting from the state of semi-war, we would waste what strength we have already built. In the end, we as a nation would fall into a crisis from which we could neither assure survival of our nation nor of the people.

As a general rule, a political system is not an end in itself but simply a practical tool for attaining goals set by the nation and the people. A genuine political democracy therefore could hardly be dependent on an unconditional imitation of the institutional trappings of any given democracy. In Korea's case, we should develop a democratic system that, influenced by our own circumstances, can best pursue human liberty, equality and happiness in a manner compatible with Korea's culture and traditions. This was also the case with the United States which, while accepting the rudiments of early European democracy, eventually developed an electoral system of its own and a presidential system of government that reflected the country's own historical experiences. As a result of such native ingenuity, America's strength has grown, its political philosophy overtaking that of Europe. Thus the United States has come to enjoy the longest history of any modern democratic institution.

What the Republic of Korea should learn from the United States is not the end-product of political institutions which were shaped by its own historic experiences, but its independent and creative spirit that helped to bring about its special system. A country like Korea, so radically removed in culture from Europe, cannot ape the European political atmosphere or philosophy, but must independently chart its own future course in accordance with its own political tradition and culture. It is our task and also our desire to create an efficient and productive democratic system, reflecting Korea's historical experiences.

A Productive Political Style

As the Republic of Korea continued to pursue its goals of modernization and national security in the 1960s, it became aware, more than at any other time, of the importance of political stability. Efforts were therefore directed at partially securing this objective. But it was not until the 1972 *Yushin* Reforms that it discovered a relevant democratic system suited to its own historical conditions and reality.

Domestic and international upheavals that began to affect the Korean peninsula in the early 1970s required a crucial decision on the part of the Korean people. With the Cold War structure beginning to shake, serious changes began to occur in the balance of the Big Powers that surround the Korean peninsula. With President Richard Nixon suddenly visiting China, Japan briskly contacting China and the Soviet Union, indications began to appear that Northeast Asia, including Korea, was once again turning into a focus of Big Power rivalry. By 1971, with the withdrawal from Korea of one U.S. infantry division in accordance with the Nixon Doctrine, the United States commitment to Northeast Asia in general appeared to be greatly reduced.

This series of developments contained an unprecedented peril to our people's survival as well as to the nation's safety. In a way, the situation surrounding Korea in the early 1970s almost reminded one of the last days of the Korean Empire a century earlier, when European Powers were similarly agitating in rivalry over Korea. At that time, it was customary for many of these Big Powers, which were bent on imposing their own order and advancing their own interests on weaker nations, to victimize smaller countries and their interests. Our people learned a painful lesson from history that smaller nations, by failing to raise the spirit of *jaju* and by becoming subservient and disunited, eventually bring on themselves the tragedy of altogether losing their sovereign rights.

As I watched the great changes occurring on the international scene in the 1970s, I felt I had to warn of the repetition of such an unfortunate chapter in our country's history. Domestically, some people, mistaking détente for the restoration of world peace, began speaking and behaving in a subservient manner by entertaining the idea of asking four or five major powers to guarantee Korea's peace and security. But under the structure of international power politics in which big powers seldom make accommodations for smaller countries, we could not allow the tragedy of the past to repeat itself in Korea by letting our complacent attitude, political quarrels and psychology of dependence reassert themselves.

With wounds from that tragedy still fresh in our mind in the form of our nation's continued dismemberment, our generation bears the responsibility for strengthening the nation's power by ourselves, for coping with these challenges posed by the outside, and for handing down to our posterity a glorious chapter in history. It is our generation's historical mission and a duty from which we should not shirk.

If these developments posed a long-term threat to our people's survival, more direct and immediate dangers came from the north Korean Communist regime which began to agitate for war. Apparently encouraged by the possibility of a Sino-U.S. détente, or its alleged contribution to peace, some people inside the nation believed and behaved as if an era of peace and negotiation had come also to the Korean peninsula. This was indeed naive and dangerous thinking.

Changes in international order are nearly always accompanied by pains and perils and such perils usually occur where realignment in international power produces a vacuum. The Korean peninsula is representative of such localized tension. Under such circumstances, it was hard to believe that the north Korean regime, which for ten years had prepared for war, and which had declared the 1970s as their decisive moment to strike, would let such a chance go by. Therefore, it was not surprising that the north Korean regime, by taking advantage of the restrictions that the Big Powers felt were imposed by the currents of the East-West détente, began slowly building tension by massing troops along the Demilitarized Zone, making Korea once again the hottest spot of tension. It was a situation in which no one could declare that war was not possible.

In the face of such turbulence and changes that threatened our security, we were the only ones responsible for insuring national survival. Informing the nation of such an unprecedented emergency, I, as President responsible for protecting the nation, its people and their property, made two important decisions. First was the opening of a dialogue between south and north Korea. Less than a generation after the Korean War, prospects of another conflict seemed almost inconceivable. To stop war, it was urgent to try to reduce tension by starting to talk. Opening of dialogue over the barriers of a generation's distrust and separation represented our nation's ardent desire to avoid another conflict at all cost. In our search for unification through peace, and not war, dialogue, also, was the first gate to enter. Secondly, in order to support the south-north dialogue and accelerate the strengthening of national power, I effected the *Yushin* Reforms on all phases of the national activity. In a time of national crisis, more important than the outside challenge itself are the people's right attitude and the nation's power to sustain itself. World history provides ample proof that national power is the only answer to the destiny of the nation. Thus, the *Yushin* Reforms were a manifestation of the people's will to strengthen the nation's power by becoming aware of their historic mission and duty.

Externally, the *Yushin* Reforms represented Korea's independent resolve to assure national survival and safety by actively reacting to international changes. Internally, it was intended to leave behind to posterity a unified Korea by broadening the basis for production and prosperity. To fulfill these missions, a great reform was launched in all spheres of national activity, including politics, economy, social life and culture. It was too multifaceted a reform to be accomplished in a short time. By trying to eradicate factors that had hampered our nation's efforts to increase power, it involved a reform of existing institutions to make them more efficient and responsive to production. Seeking to renew our national consciousness and reform the spiritual attitude of leaders as well as the general public, it also involved a quiet spiritual revolution. All in all, the *Yushin* Reforms were a creative effort designed to develop a new form of culture and tradition in Korea.

First of all, we have now fashioned a productive democratic system capable of contributing to the improvement of the nation's power by discarding the habit of imitating other countries' political systems, a habit which caused so much inefficiency and waste of our national strength. The *Yushin* Reforms, by reflecting on our past abortive experiments with a constitutional form of government, retains democracy's formality as well as its substance. But together with rights and liberties of every citizen, it defines their discipline and responsibility. Even in a situation of confrontation with a Communist regime in the north, it aims to give democracy's maximum guarantee to freedoms and basic rights of citizens. Every citizen in the Republic of Korea is guaranteed full freedom to pursue his social or economic activities, and political freedoms, including the system of multiparty representation.

At the same time, following the example of many countries around the world, acts that could imperil the nation's security or shake the democratic society's basic order, are controlled by law. Regulating part of civil liberties to protect by law a democratic order constitutes the cornerstone of any law-abiding nation; it forms the basis on which a democratic society exists. This is even more true for Korea's conditions under which such diverse and multiple goals as democracy, national security and modernization must be adequately blended.

Past experiences have taught the Korean people a painful lesson that their right to survival in peace and stability, their right to secure a decent life and human dignity are incomparably more valuable than the right to hold political demonstrations or criticize the government. How many countries in the world facing a direct totalitarian threat as we do, enjoy as much freedom and equality as we do? If the concept of freedom involves not only political freedom but also freedom for economic, social and cultural activities, then its present scope in Korea, in view of our dire circumstances, is not very much behind Europe's.

Had the Soviet Union massed its hostile arms next to Washington, D.C. or London, prepared to attack them at any minute, few would insist that average Americans or Britons enjoy more freedoms than we do at this moment. Regulating freedoms of a destructive minority to protect the freedom of the productive majority constitutes a principle for developing a democratic society. Only by disciplining the exercise of freedom could a free order be maintained and developed.

The Korean government, going one step beyond the simple guarantee of individual rights, is broadening the right to survival by introducing bold new social welfare programs. No citizen of the Republic of Korea is discriminated against because of sex, religion or social status. Every one entertains, by dint of his hard work, the hope and confidence of leading a more humane life. As the nation's power increases, so does the policy of realizing social justice. Through these policies, the Korean people are beginning to receive better guarantees for freedom, equality and happiness.

The National Conference for Unification, whose delegates are popularly elected through the democratic process and in whom is reposited the nation's sovereignty, represents the Korean people's firm consensus on the nation's established goals.

In addition to guaranteeing individual freedom and the right to survival, Korea's democratic system is also designed to attain the nation's objectives in a more efficient manner. In seeking to attain these objectives, it is vitally important to form a broad basis for consensus. A consensus is first required to create a stable political framework to prevent fruitless political strife and divisiveness over the nation's goals. Only under such stability can all efforts be marshalled for their satisfactory attainment.

Preservation of the nation's survival and safety, attainment of peace, prosperity and unification are our people's unswerving goals, the nation's unchanging objectives. These objectives cannot be the subject of partisan views of either the majority or the minority, nor can they become a bone of contention in political factional squabblings.

On the basis of such a consensus, delegates to the National Conference for Unification distill public opinion on the issue of unification and, according to the dictates of their consciences, elect the President who bears the constitutional duty to execute policies to bring about the nation's peaceful unification. In this manner, the people of the Republic of Korea can concentrate all their efforts on securing the major goals of the nation without the usual post-election unrest and political turmoil, or without wastefulness and inefficiency.

The composition and operation of the National Assembly, Korea's parliament, follow the same spirit. Unlike the past, which often saw overheated campaigns which were also very corrupt, able and conscientious people are elected through direct and indirect means. Our National Assembly, accordingly, has recovered its proper function of becoming a legislative organ whose role is to help achieve the goals set for the nation's future.

By broadening the principle of harmony and cooperation, and casting away old habits of preoccupying itself with confrontation and dissension, Korea's National Assembly has begun to create an efficient parliamentary style. In its policy debates, earnest and scientific analysis has replaced impromptu ideas or sloganeering. A worthwhile start has been made toward creating an atmosphere in which every legislator would follow the decision taken, although in debate, they would defend individual opinions. For the National Assembly to operate efficiently, it is most important for the two major political parties represented to cooperate on problems affecting the nation, but to compete fairly on political matters. Political parties in a modern democracy are expected not only to represent the interests of people who support them, but also to help shape the national consensus, and often lead it by helping the public to better understand the issues that confront the nation. If the majority and minority parties could share a common perception of the reality and objectives of the nation, and if such a perception could lead to exchanges of better alternatives, political style in general and the political atmosphere could be made to serve productive purposes.

Such a style should be developed into an organic cooperation between the executive and legislative branches. As a country's problems become more specialized and complex, it is becoming common place in many democracies for government to generate and implement more policies. In trying to cope with the socioeconomic problems of modern times, the classic division of power is becoming less and less absolute. Indeed, in some respects, it is coming to be considered even undesirable. It is against such a background that in some countries, the power of the government is being functionally integrated.

Progressive acceptance of these trends could provide Korea with an institutional basis on which the executive and legislative branches of the government could cooperate mutually and complement each other. If it is the function of the government to explain the broad goals of the nation and to seek the legislative consent, then it is the role of the legislature to reflect on the people's aspirations, and submit alternatives to the government. If it is the function of the legislature to broaden the base of consensus by ascertaining diversified public opinions, then it remains for the executive branch to seek efficient and rational ways to implement them. Such is the manner with which differing branches of the government, each with its differing roles, effectively give form to public aspirations. The emphasis in the relation between the executive and legislative branches, therefore, should be placed not so much on the principle of checks and balances as on harmony and cooperation for the common attainment of the nation's goals.

Thus Korea's political system, by blending democratic procedures with the need for efficiency, provides the foundation on which the genuine development of democracy becomes possible. To seek a stable, efficient national administration on the basis of a national consensus, democratically arrived at, and to attack the nation's goals in such a way as to benefit the people—these are qualities of an efficient democratic system and of productive politics. Korea's democratic institutions, of course, are hardly a static thing; they should be progressively designed to stimulate socioeconomic growth and to react actively to the changes of the time.

It was largely thanks to such a productive political reform that Korea was able to fulfill some of its goals in spite of the difficulties of the 1970s. In human society, however, no reform can avert the pains of change. During its early phases, some irresponsible criticism was directed against the *Yushin* Reforms, particularly by people soaked in the old habits of imitating foreign political institutions. But the absolute majority of the Korean people not only realized the Reforms' necessity and genuinely wanted and supported them, they came to have confidence and pride in a stable democratic system that was beginning to take root after accomplishing much in the 1970s. Indeed, activation of the *Yushin* Reforms helped to surmount many problems that could not otherwise have been surmounted. Most important, they helped to deter threats of war and protect national survival and safety.

If we remember the tragedy that gripped the people of Indochina in the early 1970s, we have no problem appreciating the magnitude of the crisis that confronted Korea at that time. The lesson of Indochina is that no matter how extensive outside help might be, it cannot help a nation that lacks power and unity.

For Korea, fortunately, things turned out differently with the help of the *Yushin* Reforms. The Reforms not only helped the country to overcome the crisis through the unity of the Korean people, it even promoted the efficient modernization of the country. From the postwar's largest economic crisis of worldwide recession in the 1970s, the Republic of Korea emerged with a surprising average growth rate of 11 percent per year. While the rest of the world's economies were either in the doldrums or in contraction during 1974 and 1975, Korea's economy grew by a high level of 8 percent, testifying to its vitality and adaptability.

With the power of the nation constantly increasing, so did its unity and development. The government, on the basis of such accomplishments, has been able to concentrate more time on the problem of a peaceful unification. Following the publication of the July Fourth Communique establishing the way for the south-north dialogue, the Republic of Korea strengthened its position even further with the 1973 Foreign Policy for Peace and Unification. Our efforts to find clues for reuniting our Fatherland have been subverted by antinational treachery and opportunistic provocations of the north Korean Communist regime. For all that, we have urged them to reopen dialogue.

Meanwhile, by taking advantage of the opportunities of an open society, we will continue to seek to establish our superiority over north Korea. As the Republic of Korea continues to develop economically by grappling with the trials and challenges of the 1970s, its international stature has similarly improved. Having outgrown the restrictions of the Cold War, the government has on numerous occasions declared the policy of opening relations not only with Third World countries but also with those of the Communist bloc. With a few of these, our relations have already improved. Together with an expanding economic role, these initiatives for peace have won Korea a new recognition in the world community.

Through historical legitimacy and active participation in the shaping of a new world order, we can also stimulate international conditions to favorably influence chances of Korea's peaceful unification under our initiative.

Some of these valuable accomplishments and experiences gained in the 1970s indicate that Korea's political system not only accords well with reality and tradition, but, as a productive democratic system, it is also capable of effectively solving numerous problems. After years of trials and wandering in the wilderness, Korea has at last found a genuine democracy that is beginning to take root. Although it shares the same ideological goals as Western democracies, ours functions on the basis of Korean reality and tradition.

Because our system is based on the *jaju* spirit, which helped sustain national life in the midst of many historical tribulations, we believe it has greater resilience to attack present problems; because it blends harmony and creativity, which are rooted in our culture and tradition, we believe, our system has greater potential to grow to meet the demands of our situation.

We take pride in Korea's system which we believe is capable of bringing out our nation's potential to overcome the historic partition of Korea and to realize national regeneration. That the Korean people remain fearless in the face of the planned withdrawal of U.S. ground forces is indicative of their strong resolve and confidence and trust in their productive democratic system.

May I also remind our political leaders that it is they who must bear the primary responsibility for developing their system. Because it is man who operates any institution, so it is the quality of men which determines the institution's value, which is why, more than at any other time in the past, our politicians should be sincere and honest so that they can help to create a constructive political atmosphere.

Qualities that are most expected from our politicians today are patriotism and pragmatism—an attitude, in short, of serving the people. A patriotic way of life means that politicians share pain and glory with the people by arming themselves with a strong sense of mission for their country. It is a life filled with limitless hope and confidence for the nation's future, an exemplary life ethics pursuing freedom and happiness of all the people by sacrificing personal interests. This life ethics based on devotion of oneself to the nation means forsaking personal honor and glory for the interests of the nation's future, working harder to contribute to its development.

What our country today needs is not empty theory or talk, but practical solutions to practical problems. We need wisdom and ability to shape a concrete blueprint which will enable us to gain an insight into world trends. Without such a blueprint, history can neither progress nor develop.

We should not allow acceptance of high ideals to cloud our perception of reality, nor should we become reality's prisoners by losing sight of ideals. Politicians who set the nation's goals should not assume the role of theoreticians discoursing on the philosophical reasons for them, nor should they assume the role of administrators, although it is in the nature of politicians to submit policies. By fitting their actions to goals and finding goals in their actions, politicians must always blend concrete implementation with a balanced vision of the whole policy.

That democracy is designed to serve the people is common sense. Politicians earn people's respect by sharing their life and problems; they win credibility by sharing their sorrows as well as their joys. But sincerity and compassion are hardly enough to serve the people. Service results from political decisions that are capable of solving people's problems and providing long-term benefits.

One does not expect professional agitators keen on cheap applause, or crafty unprincipled politicos gripped by greed, to solve the nation's problems and bring benefit to the country. Politicians who genuinely serve the people are those who are convinced that the policy they promote will benefit all the people; in short, they are men with courage and resolution. It is not the politician's role to play a prophet, marching ahead of his people; nor should the politician merely follow the public's whims. It is the politician's role to be a guide who can show the people the right way with patience and persuasion. Korea's political system will reveal its genuine worth and productive democracy will send out roots when politicians of high caliber gather their strength.

Ethics of a Democratic Society

The success of a given political system is influenced not only by its quality and the quality of the people who operate it, but also by the cultural and spiritual climate of the society in which it functions. Every country has its own tradition and lifestyles and when these qualities are fully cultivated, a democratic institution can take root and achieve political development.

Most people, when they conceive of political development, think of the models of Western Europe. Just because democracy and democratic philosophy originated in Western Europe, some mistakenly believed that Korea's traditional values or ethics could make no worthy contribution to democracy or to political development. But before the rise of democracy in its modern form, Western Europe was shaped by its own history and long traditions; its own political ways and styles. In the event Korea had abandoned her traditions and ethics in a blind imitation of the system of others, not only would Korea have turned spiritually and culturally subservient, it would even have risked being deprived of its own soil on which to nurture democratic institutions. Political development means a country's ability to solve its own problems, and such an ability is usually formed by cultivating potential that is concealed in its own cultural traditions.

For many years after Korea's liberation from Japan in 1945, we mistakenly believed that aping the Western European political system and style and fashion would solve our problems. By following such a mindless course, however, we lost our own merits. By recovering the traditions and wisdoms of our forefathers, however, we should try to enrich our own cultural soil, which is capable of producing our own productive democracy.

Some Western democracies, which we at one time tried to imitate, are currently in the throes of new crises and trials. In some countries, failure of the electoral process to provide for a stable majority had led to serious political crisis; in others, democracy itself has come under strain because of resurging leftist alliances that often include communists. The problem of how best to cope with the situation in which communists directly menace the roots of democratic society is now the common subject of many serious discussions in Western Europe.

I am certain that these democracies will eventually overcome their crises and further improve their system, because their institutions have so far survived many similar crises in the past. By continuing to improve their institutions, Western Europe has always succeeded in providing a stable national life for its peoples. But the fact that even some of these oldest democracies are facing repeated crises gives some serious food for thought. By correctly grasping the cause of these crises, we could avoid making similar mistakes in our own search for the development of democracy.

I tend to think that rationalism which sustained Western democracy for a long time has come under heavy strain from contemporary mass society, giving rise to an extreme form of individualism. Whenever a society is given to extreme individual or collective rationalism and when such rationalism produces fragmented individualism, the resultant conflicts and confrontation degenerate into an uncontrollable state of chaos. Attempts by individuals or groups to maximize their immediate advantage may seem rational at some point, but when seen from a social point of view, they are not only irrational but sometimes become dangerous.

It is almost comparable to drawing money from the bank because the economy is going to pieces. It would appear perfectly rational for an individual to withdraw his money if by doing so he could increase its worth. But if everybody did the same, it would not only lead to the bank's bankruptcy but even cause economic chaos. It might result in a case of individual greediness leading to collective unhappiness.

I tend to think that much of today's economic woes in Western Europe have been caused by extreme egoism of individuals and groups. A more careful examination of their situation would indicate that as a result of many conflicting organized groups confronting their governments with a rising level of demands, many countries are finding themselves under a crushing weight. Workers, entrepreneurs, consumers, farmers—each of these groups exerts tremendous pressure on the government. Many of these governments, thanks to their steady accumulation of wealth over a long period of time, may be capable of satisfying these demands, and many of these pressure groups in turn contribute, with their usual discipline and cooperative spirit, to stability and balance within their societies. With the arrival of a mass consumer society, however, rising expectations have recently become much more acute, making it difficult for many governments to come to a rational decision.

Being extremely specialized, a modern economy functions interdependently. If a railway goes on strike, the foodstuff industry that depends on transportation is affected, which in turn causes problems at the consumers' table. Such interdependence lays an entire society vulnerable to collective action by any small group. No country in the world has enough resources and wealth to satisfy everyone's demands. As a result, the government ends up satisfying one group at the expense of another.

Within the context of the breakdown of law and order, or moral decay, a situation like that could lead to chronic unrest. People preoccupied with immediate interests usually have little regard for law or morality and try to compromise or find loopholes. I venture to think that these are some of the factors that contribute to the rise of violent terrorism and communist forces in many Western societies. To cope with these social crises, many nations appeal to the restoration of law and ethics and call for the recovery of the humane qualities of harmony and cooperation. Renewed efforts are also being made to reawaken a sense of collective destiny as a way of creating consensus in society.

Against this background, the ethics and spirituality that the Korean people have inherited from their history assume greater importance in contemporary society. If we could successfully turn the crisis in Western society into an objective lesson, and thus restore our own traditions, then Korea could, without suffering the problems that afflict modern Europe, shape a foundation for the construction of a stable, productive democratic society. In this connection, in order to strengthen our collective consciousness, it is imperative to revive the spirit of *jaju* and total unity that has been formed in the course of many historical tribulations.

In contrast to Western tradition of regarding politics on the basis of confrontation between individuals and the state, the Korean people have always emphasized the relationship of harmony between the two. The word for "I" in Korean is *"na"* (individual), and the word for country is *"nara"* (state). *"Na"* and *"nara"* have seldom been considered separate concepts. Devotion to the state and patriotism, in Korea's long history, have produced many martyrs who often sacrificed *"na"* for *"nara."* From time immemorial, the Korean people, without necessarily going through the process of political party or social pressure group membership, have successfully practiced the principle of identifying individual concern with the cause of the nation.

Many of these martyrs in history, leaping beyond the barriers of partisan interests, class differences and religious prejudices, sacrificed their lives for national salvation. Many times in our history, the Korean people, tightly united around these patriots, pooled their collective energy for the cause of the nation. Such is the power of our nation's potential.

This, then, is the particular ethics of the Korean people who have never quite separated the idea of the individual and the state. By recovering this historical legacy in the form of *jaju*, the Korean people, going above partisan interests and united beyond difference of sex, religion, class and localism, are again shaping a new atmosphere of unity to strengthen the country's security, and achieve the great task of regenerating the nation.

Qualities of good citizenship, such as self-discipline and responsibility, grow from such unity. The spirit of harmony and cooperation, which grow with our idea of good citizenship, give added value to our daily life. For any open society, it is natural to experience conflicts between the government and people, between the majority and the minority, among various social groups. If looked at from the broader perspective of the nation and the people, these are but minor differences. Mutual interests and social development are served when these differences are settled from the larger perspective through dialogue and understanding. We are called upon to make greater efforts to create a society placing harmony before conflict and mutual help before struggle.

Our capacity to incorporate harmony and mutual help as part of our daily life has enabled us, despite our various disadvantages, to achieve rapid economic development and growth in all fields of endeavor. By helping to promote science and technology, our businessmen are helping to build a welfare society based on common prosperity of employees as well as employers. The new spirit of cooperation, as being introduced by the *Saemaul* movement, is helping to change our way of life and thinking. All this forms the basis of a productive democracy.

For a nation like Korea, undergoing a radical social transformation toward modernization, building a base for a stable society has a particularly important meaning. A society in transition nearly always suffers from a confusion of values. During such a transformation, it is the role of politics to shape the nation's vision and goals and to organize the people's vitality to achieve these desired goals.

Many nations around the world, whether developed or developing, experience serious pains during periods of social transformation; those failing to show their people the right path to the future suffer even deeper crises. Following liberation from Japan in 1945, Korea too was such a victim, and because politics failed to play a proper role, the word politics came to have a negative connotation. That was a logical consequence of our failure to establish a clear political goal and our failure to establish a viable ethical and logical standard to support it.

Korean politics today is no longer a simple mechanism to maintain the socioeconomic situation or effect its transformation. With the people's understanding and cooperation, it has at last recovered its role of establishing the goals of the nation: survival, prosperity and unity.

Politics in ancient Korea was hardly regarded as a means of dishing out wealth or honor; it was a creative process, producing wealth through a combination of individual and national efforts. This is how the tradition of politics based on ethics evolved. The preceding generations were so obsessed with integrity that they chose to make white the color of their national costume. Some politicians, when their honesty was misunderstood, readily gave up their lives to prove their point. If these lofty standards are revived today, politics can be saved from cheap commercialism and the base be broadened for construction of a democratic society. The wider the scale of social transformation, the greater the confusion in our value system, and the more important the role of politics. Through the establishment of morality, we can restore the credibility of the political process and through the practice of ethics we can recover the authority of politics.

The ethical and moral aspects or politics are important because no social order and no development are possible through the sole power of law. The simple concept of the rule of law is hardly sufficient. Every citizen should put it in his mind never to tamper with the law or be tempted to compromise with loopholes, no matter how small they might be.

But it takes the spirit of the law supporting its provisions to make a more humane and liberal society.

The basis for a broader democratic society could be created through the development of the traditions of harmony and tolerance, modesty and credibility, integrity and sincerity. We may accept Western rationalism, but not the ills of individualism; we may accept the concept of the rule of law, but not strict formalism. In other words, Korea should attempt to complement Western rationalism with the spirit of harmony and cooperation; our ethical strength and virtues should compensate for Western weakness of legalism. If we continue to advance both the rule of law and the rule of virtue, seeking in this process development and the establishment of a harmonious order between the individual and the state, a stable democratic society can take root in Korea. From such a marriage of Korean values and Western traditions, should grow a productive form of politics that should enable Korea to secure all the goals it has set for itself.

chapter 3
The SAEMAUL Movement and Nation-Building

chapter 3

The *Saemaul* movement being carried out across the nation is a pan-national movement designed to conquer poverty without outside help so as to build a more affluent Korea. It aims to create those conditions in which we, by first eliminating poverty and want, can lead a life of decency and culture in the midst of affluence and humanism. It seeks to leave for posterity a legacy of pride. Its ultimate goal is to create villages that are both thrifty and wealthy. This is the first step toward the goal of improving our nation.

Expulsion of want and poverty is the first step toward building a better nation. The increase of income was made the movement's primary objective on the understanding that without economic affluence, a freer and more equitable life is impossible. As the previous generation used to say, "without proper food or clothing, there can be little decorum." In conditions of abject poverty, few can display compassion or virtue, let alone decency and culture.

A good deal of our past historical stagnation resulted from poverty. In our country, attainment of objectives such as the development of political democracy, the building of a welfare state, or even the achievement of peaceful unification depends in large measure on how soon our people can lift the yoke of want and become more prosperous. It is important for the movement to achieve these objectives without help from outside sources. The principles of diligence, self-help and cooperation are a vehicle for achieving these goals.

Removing the Yoke of Poverty

Throughout the country, *Saemaul* has already made impressive gains. The picture of our farming villages, once a symbol of want and stagnation, is being thoroughly transformed. So is the Korean farmers' lifestyle and way of thinking. People who witness the impressive development and rehabilitation of Korean farming villages cannot remain unmoved. Only ten years ago, a typical scene of the Korean countryside was a collection of low, thatched roof hovels standing alongside narrow, twisted alleys. Some people might have considered it a peaceful rural scene, but not those who lived there. To them, it meant a condemnation to live with the poverty of the ages.

In the short period of less than a decade, however, that picture has disappeared. Instead, the countryside has modern villages, with farms and paddies consolidated and rearranged and people busily working their land. Flowers adorn the alleys, new wells bring forth clear water, running water is now available for everybody, and electricity is lighting their homes. Irrigation has come to the fields and paddies. In short, farming is no longer dependent on the mercy of nature's whims.

Hard work and initiative have blessed farming households with higher incomes and higher yields; for the first time in the country's history, we have become self-sufficient in rice; indeed, some rice is being exported. Per-household farming income, which remained behind that of city workers in the early 1970s, has now surpassed it. Since 1974, farm household income has been higher. If the present trend continues, it should be able to double its present level by the early 1980s. These results give us confidence that before long Korea's farming communities will reach the level of advanced countries of the world, with a healthier, more rewarding and more compassionate lifestyle.

Better than this, however, is the confidence that *Saemaul* has created in the hearts of our farmers that they, too, can shape a brighter future for themselves. Confidence is an important element for a nation stirring from a long slumber if it is to leap to progress. People lacking in confidence or ambition cannot but waste their time and thus, when occasion presents itself, are liable to be overtaken by the march of history. But a people possessing these qualities will rise from tribulations by successfully turning their misfortune into fortune.

At no time in our recent history have our farmers shown more confidence or ambition to improve their life. Their confidence and energy show the strength of their potential as an agricultural people developed over five thousand years of history. Seeing their surging ambition, which marks every village and city from the countryside to remote islands, and watching their ambition to improve their life, I cannot but be moved by their potential. The *Saemaul* movement's engine has been the people's confidence that even the hardest tribulations, once considered unendurable, can be endured given the spirit of self-help and solidarity. Given such confidence, even the nation as a whole can develop.

Equipped with such a strong potential, how is it that our farmers have so long slumbered? The answer, I believe, is that they were never given proper stimulation. The first two five-year economic development plans helped to reawaken their spirit. Long efforts and preparations went into stirring our farmers from their stagnation. Even in the early 1960s when Korea first began a modernization movement, Korean farmers lacked the preconditions to modernize themselves or the confidence to improve their life. Although their modernization was crucial to break the cycle of poverty, almost no one had the confidence or the energy to do it. The Korean farmers were simply too poor to save anything, and urban industries were not strong enough to support them. Their continuing poverty and its causes were the reason for such negativism. Too many farmers eked out their living from small patches of land; what hills and forests there were had been fully exhausted, leaving almost nothing in the way of new resources to tap.

With most of the underground resources concentrated

in the north, Japanese colonialists built their industries there, with the result that soon after the country's partition following liberation, the south was left with a traditional agricultural economy. Even what remained of the south's poor industrial facilities were totally destroyed during the Korean War. Subsequent political instability resulted in the south's cities and countryside alike continuing their way of poverty and decay.

The farmers' mentality itself was one source of the problem. Under the influence of ages of hardships and tribulations, resignation and despair became almost a way of life. Even while they were proclaiming agriculture as the essence of the universe, they lay themselves and their farmlands open to the vagaries of nature by considering natural calamities as incontrollable. Concentrating almost exclusively on growing two harvests of rice and barley, many refused to bother with experimentation with new crops, seeds or modern farming management techniques. In short, our farmers lacked courage and a progressive attitude of trying to tame nature to serving the goal of improving living standards.

While studying our agricultural problems, I came to realize that urban industries had first to be rehabilitated before a momentum could be generated to fire up our countryside. Without natural resources, experience, capital or even technology, there was of course the basic problem of how to establish a modern industrial setup. On the other hand, however, the situation in the countryside did not allow us to waste time debating empty theories, or to sit back with folded arms to wait for natural conditions to improve themselves. It is action that produces miracles, man's willpower and concerted effort that make them possible. After all, it is man who takes charge of the work of economic development. Fortunately for Korea, the country has been blessed by a tradition of a creative culture and by capable human resources. First of all, there had to be a strong national determination to achieve economic self-reliance and confidence that, given enough effort, "things do work."

The purpose of the first five-year development plan

was to awaken such determination and confidence. Its basic objective was the creation of a basis for the economy's independent growth and eventual industrialization. The first plan, thus, was a clear blueprint designed to stimulate nationwide ambition for development, to unify and concentrate public opinion behind the goal of development. Thus began our far-reaching dream of trying to create something from nothing, the objective of modernizing Korea.

To be sure, execution of the first two five-year plans was not without problems. But the basic strategy of seeking industrialization based on exports was not only daring but also relevant. The country's cycle of poverty and want, for example, could not possibly be broken by an industrialization policy aimed at poor domestic markets. For a country like Korea, unendowed by nature and saddled with miniscule markets, only an external-oriented development strategy, making full use of the abundant human resources but aimed at exports, appeared relevant.

For necessary capital and technology, however, Korea had to depend on foreign loans. At the initial stage, this policy provoked strong domestic resistance, so much so as to lead some critics to charge that the government, by drawing too many foreign loans, would eventually ruin the nation. Today, however, few would dispute the fact that had it not been for these foreign loans, our economic construction and exports would have been impossible.

Indeed, the goods we made secured overseas markets; Korea quickly absorbed modern managerial and technical skills; and the combination of these two factors led to ever increasing exports. With exports rising, and incomes of youthful workers improving, the Korean economy grew by higher rates, turning the country quickly into a modern industrial nation from its rice-growing agricultural tradition. Steady progress of the development plan helped to transform our people's way of thinking. A confidence spread in the people that if they worked hard, things could indeed improve. Such confidence was one of greatest invisible accomplishments of the 1960s.

The second important result of industrialization and urbanization was the accumulation of sufficient resources to attack the problem of agricultural modernization. Capital, technology and experience gained from export-led industrialization made it possible to expand public investment to start the modernization of farming and fishing communities. To fight droughts and floods, irrigation networks and canals were built; more plants were constructed to provide more fertilizer to the farmers in time for planting; budget allocations were made for development of manpower and for institutions required for better farming techniques.

In other words, the policy of the 1960s of sustaining a high economic growth rate was not only an end in itself, but also a means to back up agricultural modernization. That the momentum for generating rural change had to come from the city is attested to by the fact that the government, in contrast to 5 percent revenue from the countryside, had to spend 26 percent of its total budget expenditure on agricultural development.

While the government's agricultural modernization plan gained momentum year by year, it's basic supporting strategy never changed. As always, support went only to those rural projects that the farmers could not accomplish by themselves. Government support and help went either to villages that cooperated with other villages in their community projects or to villages handling projects that truly warranted official subsidies. Had government support been indiscriminate, the countryside would have been deprived of the chance to generate its own energy to modernize itself. Government support alone is hardly sufficient to modernize farming; it is possible only with the farmers' participation and self-help efforts. *Saemaul*'s spirit of diligence, self-help and cooperation are then designed to effect a spiritual revolution with which to build more affluent villages in Korea.

Whenever I have a chance, I always emphasize the theme that "Heaven helps those who help themselves." Hardworking farmers can expect to receive help from the government but not those who are indolent, to whom help is not and should not be given. Just as it is for an individual, so it is with a village or a nation: better circumstances favor those who help themselves first. Unlike other areas of industry, farming requires much more time and patience. Farm modernization or agricultural development is something that does not yield quick results. Just as one does not expect a harvest without first sowing seeds, so farming requires long hours of hard work before any results can be seen.

Individuals, like nations, can stand with their heads up only when they are determined to shape their own destiny without the help of others. Our policy and efforts in this direction have been successful. By the end of the 1960s, the Korean farmers began to display a spirit of self-help and self-reliance; soon, here and there, community leaders began to appear who had successfully coped with many trials and errors. From their examples, it became apparent that villages that acted in the spirit of diligence, self-help and cooperation succeeded with government support, but those lacking in these qualities did not, no matter how much outside aid they received.

Looking back, 1971 was an epochal year for spreading these qualities on a nationwide scale. To prevent farmers from idling away the winter months, and to keep them from gambling, the government started large-scale environmental improvement projects in the countryside. Idle farmhands were brought out to repair thatched roofs and village roads. Thus an energetic atmosphere was created. Stimulated by government support, farmers began pooling their own resources and efforts, and began attacking some long-neglected problems, abandoning their old habit of depending on the government for their every need. As these efforts continued, villages with markedly improved living standards began to appear, eventually generating a spirit of competition amongst themselves.

This was a decisive moment to fire the *Saemaul* movement.

As we reflect on the movement's success, it becomes apparent that farmers can be goaded into action more by seeing and believing what their neighbors do rather than what other countries do. Having lived in small communities for generation after generation, Korean farmers became easily resigned to their fate while the rest of their neighbors remained poor. But once they saw their neighbors rising up and improving their lives, they realized they had the potential to do likewise. A rich neighborhood always inspires poorer ones. A combination of government support and the farmers' own painstaking efforts has helped to achieve the great success of the *Saemaul* movement, producing a powerful invisible force.

The modernization of farming, which neither the earlier government-sponsored Reconstruction Movement nor the abolition of usurious debts had been able to achieve, was beginning to generate its own momentum. The task itself was of course not without difficulties. The people who actually participated in *Saemaul* had to go through unspeakable hardships quite beyond the imagination of ordinary people. Widening village roads, expansion of paddy roads, shaping new canals and fields—none of these was easily mastered. Old and young, men and women, labored and toiled day and night, season after season, soaked in mud. As I watch the shining faces of these farmers, many of whom have successfully overcome all difficulties to create a better village for themselves, I cannot but visualize the faces of victorious warriors courageously casting off their yoke of harsh poverty.

Through the successful *Saemaul* movement, farming communities were no longer a burden to Korea's modernization. In no time, they had turned into a propulsion force supporting it. A foundation was thus laid for the nation's agriculture and industry, for farm and city, to march ahead hand in hand. With *Saemaul* entering a new phase of development, its principal projects are no longer repairing thatched roofs, widening country roads or dredging riverbeds. Its projects

have now become both gigantic and much more diverse, involving the building of new, modern rural houses and the
creation of a modern countryside.

As lifestyles change and improve constantly, farmers
become increasingly capable of meeting their own needs.
They are now preoccupied with building village-owned
warehouses, mills, forests and community kitchens. Further-
more, it will not be long before rural savings will begin to be
sufficient to support the commerce and industries of the cities.
Korea's farming communities are beginning to have hope and
confidence for the first time that they, too, can match the
affluent and cultural living standards of their European coun-
terparts.

Diligence, Self-help and Cooperation

Saemaul is beginning to teach Korean farmers the wisdom required to shape a better tomorrow, and it is not by
accident that such a movement was originated in Korea. The
traditional wisdom garnered throughout previous generations
is best preserved by the farmers. *Saemaul* attempts to rediscover this wisdom and give it new meaning. The spirit of
diligence, self-help and cooperation, for example, was neither
imitated from other countries nor imported from the city. They
are native virtues that the Korean people, agrarian in their
tradition, have long cherished and practiced. Farming was not,
and still is not, possible without hard work and diligence,
self-help and cooperation. Nature, being just and unerring,
seldom rewards those who do not work patiently. The qualities
of diligence, self-help, and cooperation have been a part of the
ethics of Korean farmers for a long time, and must continue to
be so. In essence, these qualities are similar to the industrial
ethics of modern time.

Saemaul also embodies in modern language the Korean
people's tradition of a collective life. Its basic spirit to create a
better community expresses the love they retain for themselves
and for their native community. Having been exposed to

foreign invasions many times in history, a village for our people always represented a place of peace and happiness, an eternal home. From time immemorial, they have clung to the belief that life's joy and happiness are to be found in warm human relationships; such a belief has been most cherished in small farming communities. The village people are one's closest neighbors; the village itself the place of life and work. Customs such as *kye*—mutual assistance societies—and *p'umatsi*—working in turn for one another—are expressions of Korean cooperative traditions.

Strong attachments to village interests have led to powerful commitments to the well-being of the nation. Whenever foreigners invaded Korea, peasant militia were among the first to rise up to fight the aggressors. These are the elements that form the background of the *Saemaul* movement evolving into a movement supportive of national development.

The concepts of diligence, self-help and cooperation are hardly separate from each other; they are actually mutually complementary. Help, for instance, requires diligence; cooperation means you must have a neighbor helping you. These are superficially easy principles but translating them into day-to-day life requires courage, because accepting a new life attitude and new value system means nothing less than rising from old and archaic habits to seek a new course.

Diligence is a part of the work ethics in which hard work is considered the way to happiness. Man finds happiness producing new things. Not long ago in Korea, it was almost considered demeaning, under Confucian influence, to engage in manual labor. Today, however, as the country's *Saemaul* movement continues, foreigners visiting Korea are almost shocked by the hardworking and cooperative traits of Koreans. At any time and in any society, labor has been man's primordial instrument of life. It still remains the most effective weapon against want and poverty. The civilization and culture that man today enjoys are fruits of such labor.

No society that despises labor can expect to develop

itself. Man acquires diligence by finding joy in labor. The opportunities for work are abundant anywhere, anytime. In Korea's *Saemaul* movement, work may mean planting trees near a school or office; it may mean sweeping village streets, acquiring new farming techniques or management skills. Work is a delight not just as a means to an end but also as an end in itself. The joy of work is the joy of creation; a working man, therefore, is a creative man. Constant hard work and constant exploration not only bring personal satisfaction, they cause science and invention to flourish, which in turn cause civilization to progress.

The *Saemaul* movement, always moving ahead with new projects and new work, thus provides a training ground for acquiring a new work ethics. A life of diligence, when supported by self-help, yields greater results. Man becomes self-reliant only through his resolve to stand up by himself. Greater personal satisfaction and national development is assured by a life of self-help and self-reliance.

Not so long ago, Korea, dependent as it was on help from its allies, lost the spirit of *jaju*, thus becoming the prisoner of mental subservience and dependence. The *Saemaul* movement has recovered the *jaju* spirit, and the principle of self-help is once again visible in our daily life. The habit of dependence leads both a nation and individuals to a state of underdevelopment. To become more independent, every one should be more industrious, frugal and thrifty, so as to accumulate savings for the future. A nation with adverse conditions such as ours must work when others rest, must save when others spend. History teaches that people who have built affluent nations for themselves are usually characterized by the strong spirit of self-help, thrift and economy.

Likewise, the people of Korea have also stood up. Around the nation, one comes increasingly into contact with self-reliant farmers who declare that they are no longer on the receiving end of the government. When these farmers unite and cooperate, their accomplishments become even greater.

Other people have said of Koreans, "They are individually hard working and bright but collectively selfish and divisive." With some people indulging in fruitless political squabbling and dissension, there was a time when this was true. Taking a broader view of Korea's history, one finds that the traditions of cooperation and self-help were established through a pattern of collective village life, and that the Korean people have always had a penchant for tightly uniting themselves when faced by outside threats.

The *Saemaul* movement is recovering this spirit of mutual cooperation. Cooperation enhances efficiency, unity and confidence. Cooperation between one man and another arithmetically equals two men, but in substance, it also equals two men plus alpha, alpha being the factor of efficiency. It is this alpha-factor which makes the building of a bridge or the widening of a paddy road more efficient. For one man, it is a formidable job. But with two men, miracles can happen. Cooperation also enhances the sense of unity of village people. Producing a collective consciousness, it leads to amity and solidarity. Working with neighbors brings joy; collective activity results in friendship. Cooperation breeds confidence. *Saemaul* owes its successes to the power of cooperation, to the results such cooperation has brought, to the confidence such results have produced.

Not only does the principle of cooperation benefit villages and factories, it benefits the nation and people. If we cooperate by pooling our wisdom, technology and ability, there will be few things that we cannot achieve. Efficiency, solidarity and confidence originating from cooperation form the momentum for bringing about an affluent, prosperous and stable Korea.

Saemaul's guiding spirits of diligence, self-help and cooperation are thus a valuable spiritual resource, a proud legacy that can be left to future generations. They are all the more priceless because whereas material resources can be borrowed or purchased from others, spiritual resources cannot.

When these spirits of *Saemaul* are firmly implanted in our day-to-day life, then a basis for a stable democratic society will have been laid in Korea.

The acquisition of the *Saemaul* spirits has led to the nurturing of a productive democratic order in our life. In the course of solving community problems through democratic methods, a broad base for a national consensus is being achieved in Korea. A genuine democratic society rests on the principle of autonomy, and a genuine autonomy is formed by participation and cooperation by people in communities exercising self-discipline and responsibility. Various *Saemaul* projects are teaching the Korean people this wisdom of autonomy. For Korean farmers, it is almost no exaggeration to say that so far the word "democracy" has meant to them little more than election "fever" that has visited them from time to time. *Saemaul* teaches them true democracy and how it operates by allowing them to tackle common community problems.

Saemaul works this way. All village people gather to elect a leader; they decide what projects to undertake for their village; once a vote is taken on the project, all villagers, both men and women, old and young, participate in its execution. Differences of views do of course arise, but they are adjusted and resolved through debate and dialogue. When a consensus is achieved, then all voluntarily cooperate and participate. Because the participants are neighborhood friends, no conflicts arise to challenge a decision once taken. When the project fails, responsibility is taken by the whole community. Some may define this process as neighborhood democracy, or direct democracy. The important fact is that a democratic life pattern aimed at solving practical problems through autonomy and cooperation is beginning to take root in Korea.

In our short experiment with a constitutional form of government, having imitated the political democracy of other advanced countries without their historical legacy of a modern bourgeois society, the Korean people devoted more time and energy to debating about democracy and patriotism than to putting them into action. Now they are acquiring a sense of responsibility for building a better community, developing in this process a love for their community as well as for the nation. If a national consciousness means individuals' awareness of their link to the state, then people's self-awareness should be that state of mind which holds that their own improvement leads to the nation's well-being. By blending these seemingly separate but substantially interrelated concepts, the Korean people are on their way to maturity as responsible democratic citizens. Democracy is gradually becoming part of their life, not through empty theories but through concrete action and practice.

Under *Saemaul*, the community centers that are being set up in each village around the nation are village parliaments; minutes of discussions, various statistics, and documents of development projects that each of these centers keep are a record as well as evidence that democratic social developments are occurring in Korea. A base for a stable democratic society is being laid through the *Saemaul* movement, in which villagers and their leaders work together in harmony. Only people with a reputation for credibility and creativeness are elected as *Saemaul* leaders. As these leaders are from the community they serve, there is no danger of them getting involved in conflicts with villagers. The only criterion for their election is their ability to serve the village.

From ancient times, each Korean village has had respected elders around whom all the village people would gather to maintain an amicable, orderly village life. These people, without necessarily going to the ballot box, knew instinctively which person was most qualified for the job of running their village. Management of the village's collective problems, whether large or small, usually was the responsibility of these elders. Modern *Saemaul* leaders have inherited this ancient tradition. Once elected, they have an obligation to serve their village, without pay, of course, some at the risk of sacrificing their own family responsibility, which is why a

Saemaul leader, once elected, commands such respect and following from the village people.

That the abilities and enthusiasm of these *Saemaul* leaders determine the movement's success is amply proven by experience. Both in selecting and managing projects and achieving better results, villages which have able and creative leaders move ahead faster than those which do not. The greater these leaders' ability to win the confidence and cooperation of the villages, the better are the results. *Saemaul* leaders must open their minds to diversified ideas, should seek villagers' agreement and participation through patient discussion and persuasion. Because they are elected for their spirit of dedication and sacrifice, they bear the responsibility for working for the village people's collective interest in a most democratic and efficient manner.

On the other hand, *Saemaul*'s development should not depend on leadership alone. For if it is to achieve greater success, leaders must be supported by the voluntary participation and positive cooperation of the villagers themselves. Indeed, such a principle of democratic leadership is applicable not only to the development of small remote villages, but also to the development of the nation itself.

Participation and Practice

The *Saemaul* movement that originally started in the countryside has now spread to cities and factories, beginning to involve the whole gamut of Korea's national life, including the economic, social, cultural, educational and even political spheres. Progressing from its original goal of building more affluent villages for Korea's countryside, the movement, by introducing a new ethics and a productive democratic political system, is providing the momentum, promoting national regeneration.

In spirit as well as in objective, the *Saemaul* and the *Yushin* Reforms converge. If *Saemaul*'s ultimate aim rests in the creation of more affluent villages by pooling efforts based on diligence, self-help and cooperation, that of the *Yushin* Reforms is the launching of a new nation with peace, unification and prosperity by drawing on the nation's heritage of *jaju* and unity. By translating into action the spirit that moves *Saemaul*, the Korean people may arrive at the goals that the *Yushin* Reforms seeks to achieve. Conversely, by implementing the Reforms' spirit, one attains *Saemaul*'s goals.

At the base of these two movements is the necessity for Korea to effect a spiritual revolution. The success or failure of the task of national regeneration very much depends on the spiritual attitude of the people promoting it. In Korean society today, a new wind of spiritual revolution is blowing from north to south, from east to west, bringing waves of reform in the country's old lifestyle, institutions and social atmosphere. At the root of this spiritual revolution also lies our unswerving commitment to the idea of *jaju*. The *Yushin* Reforms are an instrument for us to cast aside old and archaic lifestyles and customs, but at the same time, to accept and cultivate superior and positive elements from the cultures of other countries. It was conceived to replace traditional waste and inefficiency with a productive and efficient system, to replace conflict and dissension with an atmosphere of harmony and production.

Saemaul's goal is not very different. In the place of indolence and dependence, it seeks to substitute the spirit of diligence and self-help; in the place of divisiveness and discord, the spirit of cooperation and unity. By rejecting extreme forms of individualism and materialism that any rapid economic development and urbanization are apt to create, *Saemaul* tries to seek a more humane and compassionate society that encourages love and dedication to the improvement of the collective life. This is why the *Saemaul* (New Village) is giving rise to the *Saemaum* (New Spirit) movement, another social campaign.

The campaign to promote these new spirits should not be confined to a certain area or class, nor should it end as a short-lived movement. It should be sustained and developed until a fresh spiritual and ethical attitude is firmly rooted in our national life. Pushing a spiritual revolution in any country is not an easy task, as it involves man's inner being rather than simply law or institution. It requires voluntary participation and unswerving efforts to make it successful.

In order to lift this spiritual revolution to the level of a national movement, people in various leadership positions in society must take the lead. Being in a leadership position means the capability to command influence in society. I would like to emphasize to all the people, whatever their role in society and whatever their station, that it is those in leadership positions who should be the first ones to acquire the spirit of *Saemaul*.

For the past several years, *Saemaul* education has been offered to people in various leadership positions, providing an excellent opportunity for them to perceive the significance of the spiritual revolution and put it into practice. This provides a significant chance for leading social figures to come together with *Saemaul* leaders to share experiences. Of even greater significance is the fact that once the education is completed, the participants go across the nation to disseminate what they have learned and felt.

Of Korea's social leadership class, intellectuals form the most important block of people. For any society passing through an important transition in its history, intellectuals play a great role. At a time of drastic social transformation, it is the role of intellectuals not only to prevent the confusion resulting from a breakdown of social value from being aggravated, but also to perceive the spirit of the time by watching the day-to-day events of the world. In any country and at all times, it is the role of intellectuals to grasp the nation's reality and explain it to the people, to try to pool their wisdom and ability in efforts to solve the nation's problems. By trying to reawaken the hidden potential of the people, they can also help to create the energy necessary for the development of a collective society. History has always shown that people led by energetic, ambitious and enthusiastic intellectuals advance faster than those who are not. Our intellectuals can and must make more extensive and active contributions to the efforts to attain the goal of the national regeneration by helping to cope with the many internal and external challenges and problems.

Korea's intellectuals have had a long tradition of active participation in the affairs of the nation. It was the court scholars of the *Yi* Dynasty who formed the nucleus of a literary renaissance movement during the reign of King *Sejong*. It was the tradition then for even the cloistered, rustic literati to willingly stand up and accept the call of the state when asked to do so. When Korea's fortunes were beginning to be threatened at the turn of the century by international developments surrounding the country, the intellectuals were among the first to call for a policy of strengthening the nation's defense and improving its economy to grapple with the threat. As Korea came under foreign occupation, it was they who organized and led nationalist movements for the country's emancipation. With their outlook so strongly influenced by the tradition of resistance against foreign power, however, there is a feeling that some intellectuals are incapable of reacting positively to the demands of contemporary times.

When the country was under feudalism and foreign occupation, resistance and criticism were indeed their main responsibility, and it is a tribute to their energy that many fulfilled this function so well. Many of these intellectuals offered their services to the cause of the nation when Korea became independent in 1945. On the other hand, some others, misinterpreting the currents of time, allowed themselves to be overwhelmed by a penchant for criticism and skepticism, cynicism and defeatism, negativism and rebelliousness. While some were quick to oppose and resist, they hesitated to agree and consent. While many of these intellectuals readily united against what they considered to be social injustices, they often proved incapable of making a positive contribution. The worst of these people became so negative that they considered it shameful to participate, allowing themselves to be carried away by rebelliousness and criticism for criticism's sake.

Needless to say, these negative traits hardly help the cause of national construction; neither the nation's security nor its development are served in an atmosphere in which challenges to authority or criticisms of the government draw unrestrained applause. Destruction is always easier than construction, but Korea's intellectuals should pioneer the way toward a logic of construction rather than of destruction, of participation rather than resistance, and thereby join the ranks of a creative and pioneering mass.

It often takes more courage to assess dispassionately what the government does than to try to criticize it. However, offering encouragement and hope to the people is usually more worthwhile than preaching the gospel of despair. I therefore call upon all Korean intellectuals to abandon their negative habits, which were formed under the country's ancient regime, and stop being negativistic and rebellious.

A nation's future is shaped by the confines of its vision. In other words, a people subject to a pessimistic projection of their future are condemned to live it. If a people, on the contrary, look forward to a bright future, so will they be rewarded by it. In Korea today, intellectuals have a worthy role to play to enhance courage and hope to cope with the nation's adversity, to help people acquire a proper set of values, to lead them to develop a social ethic based on the spirit of *jaju*.

The need to strengthen the spirit of *jaju* has become all the more important because Korea is currently undergoing a radical social transformation caused by the march toward modernization. Korea is an open and free society which has maintained frequent and continuous contacts with the outside world, thus it is more important than ever before to demonstrate the character of *jaju*. This *jaju* should enable us to make our social transformation serve the cause of creating a new culture and tradition. Unless we are armed with this spirit, Korea's contacts with other civilizations could lead to chaos, to a pseudocosmopolitanism, a philosophical vagabondage. This is why our intellectuals should consider the spirit of *jaju* as so important and crucial. One cannot make a valuable contribution to the nation unless he has mastered himself; one cannot become a worthwhile member of the world community without first qualifying himself as a proud citizen of his own country.

In order to minimize the pains of transformation and create a brighter, healthier spiritual atmosphere, the educational policy of the government is giving increased prominence to the subject of national identity. In this connection, intellectuals play the vital role of preventing radical social transformation from breeding decadent trends.

Even more important than this is the attitude of the people, particularly the need for affluent people to restrain their ostentatiousness. Korea's sustained economic growth has increased the number of affluent people but also widened the gap between material and spiritual culture. With more time and more money, it might appear natural for these richer people to resort to higher consumption, but if their indulgence is not restrained in time, it could pour cold water on other people's productive energy and eventually sap their commitment to a spiritual revolution. By rejecting the attitude of complacency, wastefulness and depravity that a rapid economic growth can bring, the Korean people should build a clean, healthy and brighter society.

I take this occasion to ask the country's rich to discover the genuine value of their wealth in the helping of unfortunate people by rejecting the attitude of egotism and aloofness to others. Wealth being a crystallization of many people's efforts rather than one's own work, it assumes greater value when shared. A society that puts the national interest above interests of the individual develops faster than one which does not. Our society today, more than ever, needs people who silently practice patriotism in their behavior rather than those who first scold others.

I have always asked people in public positions to set an example by their honesty and integrity. I am happy to note, in this connection, that a rising number of civil servants are receiving public respect for their faithful and honest execution of duty, in spite of insufficient remuneration. Like any other country, Korea has its share of errant officials, but these are being gradually removed through a tighter inspection system.

Even more important than the governmental restrictions is the attitude of each public official. Roots of distrust and corruption will be eliminated when public servants learn to help each other to acquire the essence of the spiritual revolution. By placing public welfare before their own, by leading lives that are more honest than others, they can find deeper happiness in life.

The significance of Korea's spiritual revolution and *Saemaum* (New Spirit) movement lies in our ability to exert ever greater efforts to improve ourselves. In the course of helping with and supporting the *Saemaul* movement, our civil servants started on the way to create a new administrative style answering the demands of social development. At one time in our recent history, many were misled into thinking that their titles allowed them to lord it over the people they were supposed to serve. By working hand in hand with farmers through the *Saemaul* movement, these officials, sharing the hardships as well as successes, are forming a new democratic ethic based on the concept of a leadership in harmony and solidarity with the people. If people in responsible positions likewise practice the idea of the spiritual revolution and propagate its aims, then tremendous energy could be generated to enable us successfully to complete the historic mission of regenerating our country.

chapter 4
Toward a New Industrial State

chapter 4

Through hard work and dedication, the people of Korea have successfully brought to a close three successive five-year development plans. They are now in the middle of the fourth plan. Its purpose is to bring the Korean economy closer to the stage of heavy and petrochemical industries, a model of an advanced economy, with the help of the experience and accomplishments of the previous plans. Among its emphases is development of a comprehensive welfare and subsidy program for the people.

In the commencement year, 1977, many economic milestones were achieved. For the first time in the nation's history, merchandise exports hit the $10 billion mark; Korea became self-sufficient in rice; and the international balance of payments recorded a surplus, also for the first time in history.

It took West Germany, one of the strongest economies in the world, eleven years to increase its merchandise exports from $1 billion to $10 billion, and Japan sixteen years. The Republic of Korea achieved that target in the relatively short span of seven years. Merchandise exports by Japan, whose economy is several decades ahead of us, reached $10 billion only in 1967. I think our people can take a veritable pride in their performance, which was accomplished by a much smaller population and economy.

In terms of rank, the Republic of Korea, at the beginning of the first five-year plan in 1962, was 72nd among trading nations of the world. However, it steadily climbed to

57th place in 1966, 44th in 1970, and 28th in 1976. With the attainment of the $10 billion export goal, Korea now occupies a proud 17th place in the global trading community, excluding the oil-producing nations.

Our economy is gradually expanding on a global scale. Koreans with their merchandise cross five oceans and six continents; we help clear jungles in Africa; our refrigerators are found in kitchens in all of Asia; Americans and Europeans are using our television sets; in cities and farmlands of Latin America, Korea-made cars are being acclaimed. In the Middle East and Africa, Korean entrepreneurs, salesmen and engineers move about briskly, building roads and carrying on business.

The structure of our merchandise exports has reached the level of an advanced nation. Thanks to our emphasis on the development of chemical and heavy industries, our commodities are now mostly manufactured domestically, the share of chemical items having drastically increased. Gone is the time when Korea's major export items were tungsten ore, squid, laver or silk. Now they are synthetic yarns, plywood, cars, ships, machinery, electronic devices and construction materials. We are even beginning to sell industrial plants abroad. Indeed, we now have hope and confidence that we too, before long, will join the ranks of the advanced nations of the world.

Energy for Economic Development

Impressed by our economic performance, some foreigners have called it "A Miracle by the Han River" or call us "Amazing Koreans," predicting that before too long, the Republic of Korea will emerge as an economic power in the world. The speed of growth of the Korean economy in the 1970s has indeed outpaced Japan, West Germany or Taiwan.

To us, however, all this is not so much the work of a miracle as the fitting results of many years of hard work to make ourselves stand on our own feet. By working hard together, we have surmounted many insurmountable difficulties. Because so much blood and sweat went into it, our progress now appears even more valuable to us.

The Korean economy, almost wholly dependent on merchandise exports, received a stiff blow from the 1973 oil crisis and the subsequent worldwide recession. Hard on the heels of the quadrupling of petroleum prices, that of the world's foodstuffs jumped many times more. Internationally, Korea's balance of payments suffered grievously; at home, prices began to spiral. To arrest a worsening balance in international payment, many advanced countries quickly enforced a tight money policy, deepening the already bad monetary crisis. Overall, their economies almost stood still for some time.

We not only wisely pulled ourselves from the shadow of this crisis, but even managed to maintain a consistently high growth rate. Even at the risk of inflation, the government, for its part, boldly continued support of production and exports. Domestic enterprises, fighting the unfavorable conditions of higher prices for raw materials around the world, did their part by briskly continuing to produce and export goods. With our engineers and workers exerting themselves even further to raise productivity and improve quality, Koreans eventually succeeded in breaking into the tight markets of advanced nations, many of which were still in a state of recession.

The pace of our growing exports, maintaining an average of 30 percent even in 1974–75, the year of a drastically reduced trading volume across the world, surprised everybody. Immensely helped by this upsurge, actual rates of growth in many sectors in the third five-year plan exceeded their originally ambitious targets, providing a firm foundation for economic self-reliance. The overall economy had achieved a base for the balanced development of all sectors, closing the gap that once existed between various industries and different regions.

While the economies of many non-oil-producing countries of the world were in the throes of stagnation, Korea, unendowed with natural resources and bound by long traditions, had won new recognition with its sustained high growth. It was a valuable experience that convinced us that we have boundless possibilities to regenerate our nation. It is also a tribute to the talents and potential of Koreans. The country has been amply blessed with a well-educated and trained manpower if not by natural resources. The time-honored respect for culture and learning that Koreans have retained, has instilled in Koreans the urge to learn and to learn well given the opportunity. This passion for education and learning reached a new peak after Korea's liberation from Japan in 1945, and the level of education now is almost unsurpassable. The government, honoring this tradition, has developed this important potential by making greater investments in education. By giving valuable instruction not only in high schools and colleges, but also during military training, the government has managed to continue to produce well-trained manpower. As a result, the quality and diligence of Korean youngsters have become a legend around the world, as can be seen by the number of medals they have won in International Youth Skill Olympics.

The entrepreneurs and civil servants who help move our economy display the same gifts and talents shown by workers. Entrepreneurs, readily accepting modern managerial skills and strategy, are determined to produce and export more. Fired with a sense of mission, Korea's civil servants, trained both at home and abroad, participate in the task of economic construction by serving as soldiers who make and execute policy goals.

Needless to say, these excellent qualities are given an ample role under a free economy in an open society. One only needs to see how the economy of north Korea, by extinguishing individual freedom and initiative, finds itself in a state of confusion. Under a closed economic system taken to its extreme, the people in north Korea are not allowed to choose the work they like or to move freely about. With people constantly being mobilized to prepare for war, free productive undertakings are almost completely stifled. The hidden potential of the people can never be released under such circumstances.

In the free society of the Republic of Korea not only is everyone guaranteed the right to free economic activity but, through friendly competition among various entrepreneurs, their aptitude and creativity are given full play. This, then, is part of the energy that fosters national development.

However, the establishment of this modernization strategy and the awakening and releasing of the nation's potential is inconceivable without the benefit of political stability. At all times and in every country, economic construction and growth becomes impossible during periods of disorder. Instability is an anathema to the concept of development and progress. We owe our capacity to successfully grapple with recession during the first half of the 1970s to our ability to meet the crisis rationally and efficiently with orderliness and discipline.

Behind such total unity is the conviction that survival and affluence depend on strengthened national power to meet the threat of war posed by the north Korean Communist regime, and that this remains the only hope for realizing the dream of one day achieving a unified Korea. It was such an unshakable unity and consensus behind the nation's goals that have enabled production and construction to go on. Such an awareness has led to the creation of a base for the stability and growth of the Korean economy.

Through these efforts, it has become possible for us not simply to oppose communism but to defeat it. In this connection, I have proposed to north Korea to accept peaceful competition between our free system and theirs to determine which system can give the people a better life. The Republic of Korea is already emerging victorious from this competition and by fully making use of our talents as a people, we should continue to sustain high growth to create in Korea an affluent, highly industrialized society.

Some are skeptical of whether the Korean economy can continue to grow at the current high rate, whether a highly industrialized society can be so quickly achieved in Korea in such a short time. The question, however, depends on our own mental attitude. If, finding smug satisfaction in what we have already achieved, we let ourselves become too relaxed, then no more progress will be possible beyond this point. If that situation comes to pass, Korea will soon be overtaken again by the even fiercer international competition that is foreseen. Our achievements so far gained, then, will have been in vain.

Maybe countries with gross national products several times larger than ours can afford to be smug about themselves, but this country that has so long struggled to lift itself from age-old poverty through blood and sweat cannot relax or delay the speed of development. If we sit down with folded arms and let pass this one chance in a thousand, Korea may not ever again have another opportunity to regenerate itself. Compared to the day we started, the results of development over the past few years are indeed impressive. But when compared to the goals of bringing about the peaceful reunification of Korea and the regeneration of the nation, they are still too insufficient. This is why the next ten years or so will be crucial for our efforts to catch up with advanced nations. Neither our present reality nor the current international situation permit us to indulge in self-congratulation; indeed, they only demand harder work to sustain the high pace of our economy.

The chief objective at the moment is to provide a better living standard and to increase welfare and subsidy programs. With many people in Korea still unemployed, a high growth policy is geared to creating ever more jobs. Nearly half a million youngsters move into the job market every year; unless work is found for them, their living standard will be threatened, and there could be a tremendous waste of our human resources. It would be almost like a river which, undammed, flows unused to the sea, generating no electricity.

Speaking of welfare policy, some appear to confuse

our policy with a Western European model which gives lifelong benefits for comparatively little labor. Saddled with the problem of a large pool of untapped labor, however, Korea's starting point in this field should be to find them work. The fullest possible mobilization of idle workers provides not only the energy for economic development, but also eventually for welfare. At a time when people are just beginning to appreciate the fruits of their hard work, our economy's key objectives should be to continue the policy of high growth, coupled with expansion of welfare and security through the creation of more jobs.

There is an even more important reason for seeking high economic growth, and that is the need for us to maintain a position superior to north Korea in our present state of confrontation. Already, the south's economic power is three times larger than that of the north, but the north Korean Communist regime, by concentrating its total resources on preparations for war, continues to present a serious military threat. Korea needs to strengthen its self-defense in order to deter threats of aggression from the north. The planned withdrawal of U.S. ground troops will place a heavier defense burden on our shoulders, as the most up-to-date arms must be developed and obsolete weapons replaced. Unless a policy of high economic growth is sustained, there will be no way to meet increased defense spending.

There are plenty of problems and obstacles in the way of maintaining a high-growth policy. The need for developing a self-reliant defense and pushing a welfare policy sometimes works against the goal of high growth. The problem of striking a balance between these conflicting aims is not easy. But as we look back over the past, Korea has managed to defend itself and build up the nation economically at the same time, even when the economy was much smaller than the present. As the scale and adaptability of the economy grow, however, I am certain that these problems will be surmounted. The Korean economy, so dependent on exports, lays itself vulnerable to the vagaries of the international market and changes in the international situation. Nationalistic regulation of natural resources and protectionism against goods from developing countries also pose serious problems. Through the analysis of long-term trends and by remaining flexible, the Korean economy should be able to swiftly react to change.

In spite of protectionist barriers raised by other countries, Korea has consistently hewn to a strategy of internationalization as a way of development. By liberalizing imports and broadening the area of exchange and cooperation with the rest of the world, the Korean economy not only achieves high growth but also makes a fitting contribution to the stability of the world economy.

As a country trying desperately to fall in step with the advanced nations of the world, we have the advantage that we can avoid the mistakes that afflicted countries that passed through similar stages of development. The disadvantages are, however, that we have to compete strenuously against them in international markets with what ability we have and face the risk of subverting our traditional values through the tremendous inflow of foreign cultures and ways. If only to maximize our freedom of choice, the spirit of *jaju* should be firmly adhered to. As it remains our objective to join the ranks of advanced nations without making their mistakes, a blind aping of Western ways will not do. The experiences of other advanced nations should serve as lessons to us, but we should direct the course of Korea's economic development our own way. The spirit of *jaju* must serve that function.

Stability, Growth and Welfare

The question of how much of an affluent society we can build for ourselves will depend very much on how capable we are of handling our future independently. The hard work of the Korean people has set the economy in a takeoff stage. The prospect is that before long the Korean people will enjoy an affluent, stable standard of living. But just as the objectives are large and lofty, so are the obstacles ahead. Just as the tempo of growth has been so quick, so the need to solve many problems is acute. Without a correct perception of reality and of the tasks ahead, and unless entrepreneurs, workers and the total population respond in unity to many of the government's policies, it may not be possible to continue the present trend of growth.

Stability is one of the vital requirements of the high growth of the economy. Stability and growth, being of conflicting nature, often produce results that are opposite to the goal; blending them to make growth in stability possible is indeed a difficult task. Unlike many other countries, Korea cannot afford to slow down its growth rate for the sake of stability; nor can stability be allowed to affect growth. Stability without growth causes economic stagnation; an instable growth threatens to produce chaos. What Korea must seek to achieve, therefore, is growth with stability and order. Stability and growth are seemingly contradictory, but in essence, they do maintain a complementary relationship. Only a stable economy makes rational distribution of resources possible; and only in a stable atmosphere do people exert their full energy to achieve continual growth. On the other hand, one of the purposes of a high-growth economy is to provide a reasonable level of living for the people in a relatively short period of time. However, even a rapid rise in national wealth, if it is allowed to shake the national foundation, cannot but reduce the significance of growth.

Let us take a look at the price system, which is often the best guide to economic stability. Steep increases in prices threaten salaried workers' real income, which in turn affects their morale. That is certainly no incentive for increased production or economic growth. Inflation also shakes the consumer order, encouraging luxurious spending and waste, eventually causing losses in resources. Rising prices also lead to weakened international competitiveness, which in turn discourages production and exports. All this is to emphasize the need for prices to maintain a proper level so that the base for economic stability will not be threatened.

Through satisfactory cooperation among the government, business and workers, the Korean economy, even while maintaining a high growth rate, has successfully coped with the dangers of price spirals. Such cooperation will continue in the days ahead, but the more fundamental roots of instability should be attacked through higher productivity and savings. A free economy, based on the law of production and consumption, supply and demand, is highly vulnerable to imbalances and conflicts that occur within the economy itself. One such undesirable effect is price spirals.

To continue the policy of high growth, it is also vital to promote the development of scientific technology and the training of manpower. Proclaiming the age of the development of heavy and petrochemical industries at the beginning of this decade, the government has concentrated efforts on the development of such strategic industries as iron, electronics, shipping, chemicals and nonferrous metals. Largely through these efforts, the Korean economy is more and more assuming the structure of advanced countries. But the share the heavy and petrochemical industries hold in the Korean economy now is smaller than the share they occupied in other countries when they attained the merchandise export goal of $10 billion. This is why the promotion of scientific technology and manpower training is so vital at this stage.

It has been customary for other advanced nations to move from the heavy and petrochemical industrial phase to that dealing with research or technology-intensive industries. By quickening the pace of the import of technical expertise, Korea should not lag behind others in this field. Advanced technology is vital not only for higher productivity, but also for improved international competitiveness.

Boundless is the limit of scientific technology. The question of how soon we can catch up with the advanced nations of the world will be determined not by the present level of scientific progress in each country but by how fast we can develop our own technology and train needed manpower. Realizing the importance of advanced technology, the government so far has done what it could to promote it, but policy alone is hardly sufficient. From now on, entrepreneurs themselves are invited to show deep interest and concern in introducing and developing new technology and in encouraging the young to acquire technological skills. In order to link technological innovation with manpower training, our society must be charged with the determination to link learning with work and work with learning. To give our young workers a better opportunity to acquire the education and training they desire is to ensure economic growth as well as welfare.

On our way to achieve high economic growth with stability, it is vital also to increase savings to accumulate the resources required for making necessary investments for higher production and economic construction. As opposed to the development of light industries which form the backbone of our present export structure, development of the heavy and petrochemical industries we seek for the future requires enormous funding and highly trained manpower. Korea should be able to provide most of the funding and to train the necessary manpower by itself. We cannot afford to squander the little savings we have managed to accumulate as a result of hard work; through a life of thrift and belt-tightening, most of this savings should be turned into investments for the development of heavy and petrochemical industries.

People producing more and receiving higher incomes naturally demand more and a greater variety of goods. Excessive consumption, however, results in resource waste and instable prices. The cardinal objective of growth with stability can be achieved by matching savings with investments. To strike a balance between the two, not only production and savings should be encouraged, our society must be permeated with the principle of thrift and rationalization. Save, but don't save what's leftover from spending; spend only what's leftover from savings. In a country so poorly endowed by nature as Korea, only by efficient management of resources can we cope with the effects of a worldwide shortage of resources.

To raise our industrial level higher and increase productivity, the creative role of business becomes crucial. Except for industries that must be held for the public interest, the government, for its part, has turned over management of as many enterprises as possible to the private sector. Even some enterprises that the government had held because of their scale are being gradually turned over to private entrepreneurs as they become capable of operating them. Under a free enterprise system such as ours, it is private business which should play the major role of managing the economy. With the government expected to further expand the role of private business, business is called upon to make greater voluntary efforts to streamline management, promote efficiency and increase specialization.

Now that many of our business enterprises have grown large enough to compete in the world, the time has arrived for them to stop depending on the government for protection and support. Through the rationalization of business practices, the improvement of working conditions and technical innovation, they should be able to improve their international competitiveness. A cooperative setup involving the government, business and the public should be able to provide the necessary impetus for growth with stability and welfare for the workers.

As economic growth has the primary objective of providing a more affluent standard of living for all, the government, with the expansion of the size of the economy, is making a corresponding effort to broaden the scope of welfare and subsidy programs for the people. As a first step toward a welfare policy, the government is trying to provide employment for those who can work. In the course of modernization many countries, as a result of an overemphasis on growth, have unwittingly, in the process, created considerable inequality. With these societies often afflicted with friction and insta-bility, economic development has been hurt. In spite of rapid economic growth, however, the distribution of wealth in Korea is perhaps better than any country with comparable limitations. As the government continues to blend welfare with growth, distribution is expected to further improve. Any country that grows rapidly is bound to suffer from temporary income gaps, and the extent of welfare policy can only keep pace with the expanding scale of the economy. This is a lesson gained from the *Saemaul* movement.

In Korea, however, in terms of medical care and other fringe benefits, we are moving more rapidly than any other country of comparable size. We have discovered that welfare, instead of slowing down growth, actually complements it. Here is a field in which we have let our ancient traditions of *jaju*, harmony and creativeness take hold. What Korea needs is a welfare policy based on reality and on our particular stage of development. Korea cannot afford to blindly ape the income or welfare policy of other advanced countries. Should we ex-pand welfare in disregard of reality, it would only dampen the enthusiasm of some hard-working people. Should welfare pol-icy, in opposition to its goal, encourage indolence and a psychology of dependence among some people, it would have harmed not only development, but also welfare. No matter to what degree civilization develops, a society of idlers will never materialize. Even if it did, it would be a highly undesir-able phenomenon. The society we all seek to create is a society in which people will find delight in just labor, taking just reward for creative activity rendered.

The Factory *Saemaul* Movement has resulted in many successes in increased productivity and welfare. Its concept is to bring both the employers and employees a better living standard by creating an atmosphere in which they trust each other and depend on each other. By improving the physical conditions of the factory and the treatment of workers, it seeks to bring both the employers and employees a common prosperity. The ancient tradition of harmony and cooperation is brought to bear on the factory.

One of the most important ingredients of a successful business is the creation of those conditions and that atmosphere that would elicit the maximum loyalty of workers to their employer. He should be able to see that his employees are given the attention they need to lead a humane life and have hope for the future. If workers are treated like members of a large family, their response will be a quick identification of themselves with the factory. Also by returning a part of the profits for the benefit of the workers, an employer is rewarded with greater efficiency and productivity. It is this spirit that moves the Factory *Saemaul* Movement.

Instead of focusing on immediate gains, entrepreneurs and workers are called upon to maintain an atmosphere of amicability so that on the basis of fraternity and humane dialogue, they may develop an ideal working relationship. Thanks to the Factory *Saemaul* Movement, it is gratifying indeed to see a warm labor-management relationship forming in many offices and plants. The morale of workers has been raised as a result of employers building dormitories and night schools; the *Saemaul* movement has helped to create an atmosphere within which a unique relationship can now hold true. Through the unity of employers and employees, through a drastic improvement in productivity, the *Saemaul* movement has turned into an engine accelerating the pace of economic development and strengthening national power.

Such native wisdom should be applied to other areas of national activity, if only to avoid the ills and undesirable side effects that afflict other countries similarly seeking a high degree of economic growth. Drawing on such native wisdom has always been essential for less developed countries trying desperately to catch up with advanced nations of the world. It is also here that the strength of native creativeness is being tested.

Another example is our environmental protection campaign. Around the world, almost every country is suffering from the effects of contamination and the pollution of the environment. Conditions for life are turning from bad to worse with more and more mountains and rivers becoming polluted by industrial waste. Enormous amounts of money are being poured into stopping this trend, so much so that some economies are being slowed down because of a preoccupation with fighting pollution.

Our problem is not yet so acute, but the government is taking steps to prevent the encroachment of industrialization on nature. In our efforts to preserve the beauty of nature, it is not so much propaganda and sloganeering that are effective as it is concrete action growing out of a love of nature itself. If we begin now to conserve and beautify our natural surroundings beginning close to home, the country will not be forced later to mobilize gigantic efforts in haste to protect the environment. No matter how great man's skill to create everything artificial, he cannot survive apart from nature. If the Korean people, in unison, start an environmental protection movement now, the country will see both industrialization and a pleasant environment coexisting side by side.

If the government, business, workers and the rest of the population pool their intelligence and efforts, the building of an affluent society with welfare will not be far away from us. If only the current trend of high growth with stability continues, the country's living standards will reach those of advanced nations by the 1990s.

One of the most important things to do now is to carefully watch the trend in other countries, to fix a clear vision for our future. In some phases of our long history, because Korea allowed itself to be overtaken by other nations, it was condemned to poverty and stagnation. As a nation, however, Korea has always had a strong potential to reassert its indomitable spirit of *jaju*, harmony and creativeness. If we can draw on this potential again, gain a correct perception of changing world history and wisely react to these changes, then we will succeed in shaping for ourselves a highly industrialized society. Then, people who live in Korea will find the affluence and welfare they seek. They will be blessed by clean mountains and clear rivers and by the customs they have so long preserved and enjoyed.

Toward a Compassionate Society

One of our goals is to create in this land a nation not only materially affluent but spiritually healthy, a society which is ruled by the spirit of fraternity and compassion. While the pursuit of the advantages of modern civilization and the comfortable life it offers remains our goal, we must not overlook the importance of creating a society preserving valuable traditions and customs, in short a society in which compassion rules. What we desire is a highly modernized society without the usual ills that are displayed by other advanced nations.

The causes of problems that normally accompany modernization or industrialization should be thoroughly examined well in advance of their arrival. Examining the problems of other advanced countries, we find at their roots the problem of dehumanization. A highly industrialized society is a society extremely mechanized, specialized, organized and rationalized. Ironically, however, the more complex society has become, the more unhappy and fettered has become man's lot. In the shadow of a highly mechanized civilization, man has turned into a slave of machines and materialism, with his individuality and personality lost in the organization. With mass society taking over, fraternity and compassion disappearing, man finds himself in increasing alienation and loneliness. Take the case of shoe manufacturing, for instance. A shoemaker who handles all the work attendant on making a pair of shoes may be moved by a feeling of accomplishment. But not so he who is reduced to making the same part day after day in a dreadful factory routine. He who does so is a victim of drudgery, powerless before the machine and lonely within himself.

Modern man, under such circumstances, is apt to lose control of himself, easily becomes the victim of excessive consumerism, his value system turned upside down by the onslaught of consumer culture. He is then swept away by the force of fads and fashion. Reeling under a daily bombardment of advertisement, everyone is literally pushed into buying new and ever newer products. One finds oneself a prisoner of fashion, aping other people's lives and other nation's standards of living. The more materialistic a society becomes, the more prominent is this phenomena.

It is natural for people enjoying an increasingly better life but struggling under the pressure of an industrial society to seek the comfort of modern civilization and the amenities it offers. Under no circumstances, however, should material wealth be allowed to become a standard on which to judge human or social values. The idea that money answers all problems, or the attitude of flouting compassion and faith in pursuit of material rewards not only destroys spiritual life, it threatens social equilibrium and harmony by negating individual social discipline. If such a materialistic tendency is compounded by individual or collective egotism, people eventually forfeit their sense of belonging.

The plethora of organized activities in an industrialized society may give the semblance of frequent human contact and exchange. But with most of them likely to be associations based on narrow professional interests, modern society in fact turns into more of a theater of barren competition. With a variety of different weltanschauungen and other value systems competing for attention among different generations, races, classes and professional groupings, solidarity in its broad sense within society has become almost untenable. In urban day to day life, family units have become smaller and smaller with friendship circles ever narrowing. Loneliness and nihilism cannot but be bolstered.

How does one explain the fact that the suicide rate is usually the highest and the number of psychiatric patients largest in the most civilized and advanced of countries? The question only underlines the barrenness of materialistic and individualistic society. Imagine the picture of aged couples, abandoned by their children, lonesomely strolling in parks, or unwanted children, neglected by their divorced parents, and you have the causes of social tension and instability, with the attendant phenomena of juvenile delinquency, rebellion of youth, increased criminality, confusion, and psychological instability. Youngsters turn to decadence and to growing their hair long, desperately trying to fill a spiritual vacuum. Some of these ills may seem inevitable, and the question would be how better to cope with them. The answer may depend to a large degree on the strength of the individual or social values a country has, or on the texture of its spiritual culture. Take the case of a poor family suddenly turning rich and finding itself unhappy. In this case, it is not so much the wealth itself as the family's failure to cope with it that is the cause of unhappiness. With every one making his choice as to the meaning of happiness, defining it becomes even harder.

For all that, there is something universal about man, making it not impossible to find a common standard. Convenience in life is sought, as well as survival and safety. Indeed, it is to free the people from the yoke of poverty and provide them with greater material affluence that economic growth is sought. But a materially affluent life alone hardly guarantees happiness, for things in themselves can never produce it.

Man develops a liking for or an abhorrence to things that he sees, hears about or feels. We react the same way to family and neighbors. It is said of man that he is a social animal, which means he cannot live apart from others. Either in human relationships or in doing something good for others, he craves respect and fulfillment. By sharing poverty with fellow neighbors, or by seeking common development rather than individual wealth, one may find deeper satisfaction and happiness. Others, out of their love for community or for their nation, gladly offer their lives. A society's soundness is measured not in terms of the number of high-rise apartments or the efficiency of its traffic system, but by the amount of its compassion and humanity.

In many advanced industrialized countries, a growing number of people are beginning to talk about the recovery of humanism. They are talking about stronger value systems and deeper spiritual beliefs, warmer human relationships and more communication within families and communities.

In the advanced industrialized society we seek to achieve for ourselves, Korea's traditional concepts of harmony and cooperation should be strongly established and even more brightly manifested. Some Westerners are beginning to show interests in our ancient ways and wisdom, some even getting immersed in the study of Korean religions and philosophy. This should be a source of encouragement.

Korea has not yet entered the stage of having to worry about the innumerable ills that afflict other advanced countries. However, we do see, from time to time, how beautiful native customs and ways are being eclipsed by the shadows of urbanization; or how fads and fashions try to overtake the reality of our society. The more common such trends become, the stronger should be their assertion of *jaju* and of our self-identity. It should be Korea's ultimate aim to blend Western modernism with Korean traditional culture and values so that, out of such a marriage, a new society free of the familiar ills of industrialization can arise.

The higher our economic growth and the more sophisticated our civilization becomes the larger, rather than smaller, should be man's place in it. Unless human dignity is given its rightful recognition, material civilization is as good as dead. So it was in the Renaissance movement in the West, which began with an attempt to recover mankind from medieval darkness. That was how the study of ancient man and his thought began.

As Korea prepares to greet the opening of an advanced industrialized society, it should attempt to give greater effort to reviving the wisdom and spiritual traditions of the past, for what we seek is not just the façade of an advanced civilization but a truly livable society in which material affluence will go hand in hand with humanism. It should be a society of mutual development based on compassion and cooperation, but not one rent by conflict and struggle; not a society decaying with decadence, but one ruled by respect for honesty, sincerity and industry. Instead of being overly competitive, tense and lonely, our life in such a society should be relatively stable and happy.

By making expression of sympathy almost a virtue, the Korean people through the ages have cherished the tradition of helping the less unfortunate. To see how this tradition still lives, one need only watch the reaction of the general public to each natural calamity or manmade disaster. Almost instinctively, they rush forward with aid ready to help with rehabilitation. Never unmoved, victims rise from the rubble to make a fresh start.

As another example of our strong spiritual tradition, one may cite the parent-child relationship in Korea. Foreigners who come to Korea for the first time marvel at the custom. Here, no children would dare send their aged parents to an old people's home. The number of old people's homes is certainly not in Korea considered a good mark of the social welfare system. The sight of neighborhood people helping the aged is commonplace in Korea. When such a beautiful custom permeates society, the proper atmosphere for maintaining warm human relationships is created even in the midst of an industrialized society. A relationship based on trust, whether it involves teacher and student, old and young, or employers and employees, should be the guide for all associations.

The *Saemaul* movement is an excellent guide for the creation of a society of genuine compassion. *Saemaul* villages are not simply villages or administration units but entities of cooperative life where national traditions are harmonized with modern civilization. Inside factories, office rooms, schools or on the farm, the spirit of the *Saemaul* movement should create a balance. In a country undergoing Korea's scale and speed of change, this spirit assumes an especially significant importance.

As in every other city in the world, Korea's urban life, in Seoul as well as in other cities, is becoming increasingly characteristized by indifference to neighbors. If our urbanites succeed in leading a healthier life and still manage to control the amenities of modern civilization, cities in Korea will make the positive contribution of becoming windows through which foreign cultures are successfully absorbed and distilled.

Not only through the *Saemaul* (New Village) but also through the *Saemaum* (New Spirit) movement, life in our cities is becoming a little more healthy and compassionate. Discarding the old habits of waste, distrust and discord, ushering in a pattern of thrift and diligence and harmony, more and more people are becoming a little more sensitive to their neighbors' needs. Surely, the society we are on the way to building should not be just a collection of fragmented individuals; its mark should be sincerity, credibility and fraternity. By preserving compassion and morality, it should be one in which man will be allowed to control things.

Given the present tempo of growth and a definite vision for the future, I am certain that, by the 1990s, Korea will have built a society of affluence whose citizens will not envy the life of other countries. Per-capita income of Koreans will have reached the level of advanced industrial countries. Our exports will rank among the highest of the world.

When that time comes, citizens will be able to choose the work they like, demand compensation justly reflecting their labor, and fashion for themselves a future bright with hope. Whether in the city or on the farm, people will be freed from the need for the basic necessities of life and enjoy the benefits of modern civilization. The children of Korea, with the opportunities for advanced education wide open, will then pursue their studies without worry about jobs or tuition. They will then show the world their talents as a people with a long tradition and history.

Korea's lands will have turned verdant, "the field of ocean green" as once proudly described by our ancestors. The face of our country will be crisscrossed by expressways; nearly every part of Korea will be within a day's distance. Seoul and other large urban centers, laced with industry and farming, forest and resorts, historical sites and natural surroundings, will be a beautiful picture of balance. New cities will rise alongside factories, lands that no longer thirst for rain will form the suburbs, and the countryside will be dotted with pretty farm houses. Gaps in income or cultural standards will be unknown. Korea's ancient culture will flower. Together with rehabilitated historical sites, the well-preserved environment will present a fresh image of a vibrant Korea. To meet the requirements of a modern age, healthy mass entertainment will satisfy everyone's emotional needs. Beyond all this, Korea, while becoming materially affluent, will not have lost its tradition of compassion. It will have turned into a brighter country, its long spiritual culture soaring and flowering.

chapter 5
Korea in the World Community

chapter 5

While pursuing the goal of creating a highly industrialized society, Korea must also actively and wisely cope with the changing international situation around her. The attainment of political stability and affluence is important in itself, but in the midst of international turbulence, it should be made an instrument for ensuring the nation's survival and continued stability and the means through which Korea can strengthen its independence to achieve peace and unification.

Having gone through the Cold War phase, today's international community is undergoing an important transition, posing unprecedented challenges and tribulations for Korea. The bipolar structure of the world, in which the United States and the Soviet Union held mastery over other nations, has been slowly disintegrating. As to what new order will replace it, or what influence this phenomenon will have on the Korean peninsula, few are capable of predicting. The current turbulent state of affairs is still in the process of evolution; its outcome will depend very much on the choices and decisions that many countries, including our own, will be called upon to make.

Changes in the international situation offer risks as well as opportunities. People who correctly perceive the risks behind the changes and determine the ranges of choices offered by them by swiftly reacting to new circumstances can expect to broaden their freedom of choice. If, however as our recent history would indicate, we fail to perceive the nature of the changes that are taking place in the international order and fail to react in a fitting manner to the demands of the new circumstances, then not only will we lose the freedom of choice preciously given us, but we might even find ourselves falling behind others in the international community. By making good use of valuable historical experience, the reality behind the international political situation should be correctly perceived, and from that vantage point the opportunity of attaining the nation's dream of reunifying Korea can be explored.

Korea must wisely cope with the challenges and trials that the international situation presents, with the sense that the Korean people are not only masters of the peninsula but that Korea is a rightful member of the world community. As Korea's role enlarges around the world, the nation should be able to perceive not only the changes occurring in northeast Asia, but also the long-term trends and their intensity. The time has come for us to improve our adaptability and quicken our progress in an effort to project a new chapter on world history, a chapter of national regeneration and unification. Most important of all, Korea is called upon to unify itself through peaceful means, and through unification to make a fitting contribution to world peace and prosperity as a proud member of the global community.

From Peace to Unification

In response to the aspirations of the 50 million people of all of Korea and the demands of their five thousand years of rich historical tradition, we owe a solemn duty to history to rise above the tragedy of division and open a new epoch by reunifying our Fatherland. But the road leading from division to unity, for us as well as for others, is strewn with many difficulties and challenges. As always, unification of territory hardly comes as a gift; it is a national undertaking of a grand scale, a great historical event, the accomplishment of which must be won through arduous preparation. It requires a grasp of the logic that created the division, the long process of the formation of a determination to unify, and the pioneering task of creating a new order beyond the hurdles of heterogeneous ideology and social system. It also requires the formation of a realistic unification formula by carefully guarding against the tendency to forget the tragic meaning of division or to take it for granted. In order to unify Korea, the nation must conserve its innate strength, steadily endeavor to create conditions conducive to unification, and be prepared to quickly seize the chance when it comes.

Depending on how one looks at it, the goal of unification is both far and near. It would be far indeed if we resigned ourselves to thinking that the country's division was the work of the Big Powers, and we could not do much to overcome it. Then and now, with their differing interests, the Big Powers cannot be expected to come up with an easy agreement to solve the problem of Korea's unification. On the other hand, if we determine that the tragedy of division was due as much to our own lack of *jaju* strength as to the work of the Big Powers, and should we then concentrate our active endeavor for its dissolution, the goal of unification cannot be far away.

Needless to say, we Koreans never asked for this territorial division. On the other hand, however, although it was the result of an overwhelming international situation of the time, Koreans should also share part of the blame for having failed to prevent it. In my random reflection on Korea's recent history, I believe that the chance to avoid the tragedy was never really completely denied us. In the jubilation over Korea's liberation from Japan's colonial rule, Koreans from all walks of life failed to pool and unify their national determination to make a fresh start as a unified, independent nation. Some of our own nationalist leaders may have to share part of the blame, also, for failing to perceive the real intentions of the Big Powers and for hastily and naively equating emancipation from colonialism with the automatic birth of an independent nation.

The fundamental blame for the division, of course, should go to the alien ideology of international communism, and the north Korean regime which subscribes to it. Had the Communists in the north, soon after Korea's liberation, responded to the nation's wish for independence and opposed the trusteeship for Korea, the foundation for eventual unification could have been laid. At the behest of the Soviet Union, however, the Communists chose to divide the nation by overnight changing their original opposition to the idea. From that time on, they began to conspire to occupy the north.

Their ulterior motive became evident from November 1947 when the United Nations, succumbing to our opposition to a trusteeship over Korea, resolved to hold an all-Korea election, both in the south as well as in the north, under its own supervision, and dispatched the U.N. supervisory commission. The Communists not only refused to allow its entry into their territory; they began quickly building an ideological wall across the 38th Parallel to divide the nation. In the face of this development, the nationalists in the south were forced to abandon the idea of coming to a compromise with the Communists. Their only choice was to launch an independent republic in the south. In taking this course of action, they realized that a compromise with the Communists was impossible and that they would first have to establish the nation's legitimacy by establishing an independent country and then wait for eventual territorial unification.

But the Communists had not quite exhausted their repertoire of acts betraying the cause of the nation. On June 25, 1950, they started a war that reduced the entire country to rubble, a tragedy seldom seen in the annals of Korea. It was a war that also showed that the north Korean Communists cared more about their alien ideology than about the cause of the nation.

Although the roots of aggression are buried in the Cold War, the hot war had the effect of intensifying the Cold War. By making Korea a Cold War symbol, the Communists had actually reduced Korea's freedom of choice and limited its option. Korea continues to remain divided, and because of territorial division, our country, despite its long history and tradition, has not been fully accepted by the community of nations.

Now as then, the existence of the north Korean Communist regime poses the last serious obstacle to unification. Turning their back on the preponderant aspirations of the nation, the Communists not only prepare for another aggression against the south; they are frantically trying to destroy Korea's ancient traditions and lifestyles and by attempting to create a new society for themselves are forcing heterogeneous ways on the nation. They preach the gospel of class struggle in the name of Marxism-Leninism and try to impose communism on the south by force and violence. Although they pay lip service to the spirit of *jaju*, peace and the unity of the nation, in reality they commit acts contrary to these spirits. In other words, the Communists stand publicly for division and struggle rather than unity and cooperation. While they speak of peace and order, they actually agitate for war and revolution. By trampling on the ancient traditions of respect for and cooperation with neighbors, the Communists are trying to stifle the notion of showing loyalty to one's nation and faith and kindness to kin.

As the most doctrinaire and destructive of all communist parties, the regime in the north is now on its way to wiping out all traces of the traditional cultural legacies of Korea, and desperately inculcating in the young a distorted and doctored version of Korea's history based on the philosophy of class struggle. Communism, needless to say, is not compatible with Korea's traditional spirit or culture, and if only to preserve and develop the nation's legitimacy, communism in the north should be repulsed and defeated. No matter how credible their slogans or propaganda may appear, so long as they cling to the concept of class struggle and refuse to restore our national spirit, they are not likely to give up the idea of unifying Korea by force.

By trying to export revolution not only to the south but to many other countries around the world, they have also brought ignominy on Korea's honor and prestige. Their aggressive nature makes unification not only crucial, but also hard to achieve. All this requires that the question of unification be thought out in the most cautious terms, beyond the level of sentimentalism or wishful thinking, for it involves not only the question of *why* it must be attained but also *how*.

A homogeneous people, unnaturally divided, almost instinctively cries out for unity. From the standpoint of history, Korea remained one nation for thirteen hundred long years after *Silla* unified the rival kingdoms. Of the countries divided as a result of World War II, the passion for unity has been most strongly felt by Koreans. Germany remained unified for only seventy years of its history, China's concept of unity has always been diluted by a diversity of races. It is only natural for the Korean people, now divided into south and north, to try to recover and restore their self-identity as a nation with a long cultural tradition.

From the standpoint of the people themselves, the division and subsequent war have split the members of millions of families from each other. It goes against human nature and against Korea's long traditions of upholding compassion and brotherhood to erect this artificial wall just a few kilometers away and to continue to prevent these families from being reunited with each other. The mental distance between the south and north must now be greater than the breadth of the Pacific Ocean. At the very least, our desire now is to allow the members of the divided families to be able to see each other and exchange visits, if possible. Indeed, with the north Korean regime seriously bent on destroying the time-honored traditions of Korea, it has almost become our sacred duty to allow the sixteen million fellow brethren in the north, who are constantly being pressured to accept a foreign way of life and culture, to share our joy of freedom and material affluence.

From the standpoint of the nation, Korea is destined to

ensure its survival and prosperity in a fierce rivalry involving our formidable neighbors—1 billion Chinese, 240 million Russians and 100 million Japanese. If only to prevent the waste in human and material resources that results from a continued state of division and conflict and thus to display our full potential as a nation, unification is indeed most urgently desired.

From the standpoint of the international situation, a Korea unified would have eliminated one of the most tense spots in the world. By becoming one, Korea could make a positive contribution not only to peace in Northeast Asia, but also in the world. Although a small country of only 50 million people, Korea, reunified, could emerge as a strong nation, capable of harmonizing relations with neighboring countries, and becoming an effective guide to a firmer peace.

The need for Korea's unification is based on such a genuine aspiration and clear definition of objectives. And these are the reasons why our unification formula should not become vulnerable to proposals based on sentimentalism or adventurism. In other words, we should guard both against the attitude of resigning ourselves to the impossibility of unification and against the theory that it should be attained whatever the costs. What we need is a strong willpower that does not succumb to adversity and a cool logic which does not panic at the occurrence of dramatic changes in international society. Such determination and attitude should take us, step by step, toward the goal of stable unity.

The direction of our policy is contained in the "Three Principles of Peaceful Unification." First, it calls for peace on the Korean peninsula and, to make this possible, the signing of a nonagression agreement between the south and north; second, it calls for steady progress in the south-north dialogue to recover mutual trust and credibility; third, it seeks to broaden and diverisfy exchanges and areas of cooperation leading eventually to complete opening of each society to the other. When both sides have opened their societies and achieve a certain level of homogeneity through these preliminary steps, then a free election, to set up a unified government, could be held, in the south as well as in the north, according to the proportion of population.

Needless to say, it is peaceful unification that we seek; not only does this policy reflect our nation's ancient peace-loving traditions and the spirit of nonviolent pacifism manifested in our March First (1919) Independence Movement, it accords with the unification's final goal of making a worthy contribution to the cause of world peace. Even to this day, the destruction of the Korean War underlines the preciousness of peace in Korea. With the destructive power of modern arms becoming ever more frightful, the result of one more war will cause unimaginable calamity. What meaning would unification have, if what we united was just a heap of debris? Only through peaceful means could the goal of unification coincide with the nation's objective of bringing about development and prosperity.

No less important than peaceful unification is unification based on the spirit of *jaju*. It remains our firm position that any formula dealing with the Korean question should take into consideration the freely expressed aspirations of the Korean people. Just as an independence given by others is incomplete independence, a formula imposed upon us by others could not be perfect. Unification, ultimately, is a question that we must solve by ourselves, because we remain the chief parties concerned, and herein lies the reason for our continued call for restoring mutual credibility through expanded dialogue and exchanges. It may not be possible to stop the Big Powers or Third World countries from playing the self-imposed role of honest brokers, but to wholly depend on their help—which would mean the reemergence of a subservient attitude—goes completely against the goal of seeking the independent development of our country.

The Republic of Korea also seeks democratic unification by means of peace and independence because through the process of territorial division and subsequent war, the Communists in the north have revealed their antinational and antidemocratic nature. A proposal for a free general election involving both the south and north has been submitted in order for the 50 million people of Korea to freely express their feelings in the launching of a unified government. In whatever form or substance it takes, any formula which goes against the principle of allowing the people to freely express their position can hardly be called democratic.

The theme of peace and *jaju* and the goal of democratic unification are expressions of the national spirit which have been carried on over five thousand years of history, and through which we have inherited the historical legitimacy of the nation. For a long time the Korean people have upheld the spirit of peace, *jaju* and democracy by sharing life and death together; they have built up the nation's potential which has helped to deter so many aggressions by our neighbors in the past. These spirits also form a powerful national consciousness that cannot be easily extinguished by temporary occupation or dismemberment of our land.

Unfortunately in north Korea today, as a result of the attempt by the Communists to destroy the traditional way of life there, considerable signs of heterogeneity are beginning to appear, so much so that some thoughtful persons, worried by their effects, tend to be skeptical of the possibility of restoring traditional harmony and order even if the country were reunified. However, I cannot subscribe to the theory that our nation's abiding spirits, forged through many thousand years of time, can be snuffed out by a few decades under communism.

Once Korea is reunified under our leadership, the wounds of division should be healed through our collected efforts, and I am convinced that the Korean people, by restoring their identity, will be able once again to show their true selves. Indeed, herein lies the reason for us to strengthen our hand to seize the initiative for unification, on the basis of our national spirit, by fighting all adversity.

In our efforts to achieve these goals, one of the most urgent questions is how to anchor peace on the Korean peninsula, for peace is the first step toward achieving the goal of a unified Korea. To believe that unification is possible without peace is a delusion. And the peace we seek is not just a passive peace based on the absence of war. Ever since the Korean Conflict ended in a ceasefire in 1953, the clouds of war have never really been cleared because of the never-ending military provocations by the north. The significance of peace should therefore lie in the creation of a positive peace in which all threats of war have been clearly eliminated. By agreeing to sign a nonaggression agreement, north Korea should show, by deeds rather than words, its willingness to abandon war as a means of unifying the country. It should also respond to our proposal for exchanges, cooperation and dialogue by casting away its long image of bad faith and hostility.

The 1972 July Fourth Communique was a significant milestone in bringing the two sides together beyond the barriers of different ideology and system. Once again, however, by rejecting our peaceful and independent efforts to come to terms, the Communists in north Korea turned their backs on the nation's expectations by digging underground tunnels for clandestine aggression and by committing military provocations. These were signs that as yet, they were not quite prepared to abandon the policy of unifying the country by way of force.

The attempt to bring peace through dialogue and cooperation will not just end with elimination of the danger of war, but will even become an effective guide to achieve unification by ourselves. We guard ourselves against a subservient policy such as the proposal to seek a Big Power guarantee for Korea's unification because of the possibility that it would lead to a consolidation of the status quo, and thus weaken the chance of unity. This is why we consider the opening of dialogue and the signing of a nonaggression agreement to be the first steps. The gate of unification opens through expanded exchanges and cooperation.

These positive steps to bring peace are all the more necessary to stop the social and cultural heterogeneity between the south and north from growing worse. It is to prevent such heterogeneity and to encourage restoration of the nation's homogeneous character that we have called for exchanges and cooperation in areas that are most practicable. In order to clear away the differences that have accumulated for three decades and recover the nation's spirit and preserve its cultural traditions, ceaseless dialogue and exchanges are necessary between the two sides; the establishment of peace is therefore a precondition for restoring our homogeneity.

Put succinctly, our policy is peace first, unification second. In other words, it seeks to create conditions conducive to unification, step by step, on the basis of peace. It seeks to spare the Korean people from another destruction of life and property which would go against human morality; it attempts to respond to the solemn call of history to eliminate once and for all the fear of another war. It is indeed a sorry picture to see the north Korean Communist regime refusing to accept these offers.

But we shall not easily despair. In spite of their continuous armed provocations and barbarity, we have held steadfastly to our unification policy of tackling practicable measures first. They include the signing of a mutual nonaggression agreement, simultaneous entry by the south and north into the United Nations, exchange of visits by members of families on the occasion of the *Chusok* (Korean Thanksgiving) holiday and economic cooperation between the two sides. Our effort to get the north to accept these proposals will continue steadily.

On the other hand, with the north rejecting these offers and continuing its policy of war preparations and military provocation, we must be ever ready. There is only one way to destroy the north's delusion of unification by force, and that is to strengthen the Republic of Korea. When the north realizes that the south could neither be conquered nor subverted from within, that will be the time when the Communists will change their minds. In order to block their armed provocations and open the door to unification, the south's military, economic, social, and political strength should easily overwhelm that of the north. I am certain that the north will become more appreciative of our proposals of a nonaggression treaty and dialogue when it begins to realize the extent of our strength, both internally and externally.

However, even the slightest indication of dissension or unrest in the south will be quickly misunderstood by the north as weakness, and perhaps lead to a miscalculation, inviting, in the process, their familiar strategy of a subversive united front. This is a familiar tactic. And herein lies the need for showing the north not only our expanded strength, but also a national consensus and total unity behind the government.

If the Republic of Korea continues to seek development with unity, I am certain that history will be on our side. Nowadays in Eastern Europe, more and more voices are rising to demand political liberalization. They appear to be steering toward an independent course, by reflecting on communism's own limitations and by challenging the supremacy of the Soviet Union's position in international communism.

North Korea, even with all the trappings of a garrison society, will not be able to swim against this current of liberalization in the communist world. The advantages adhering to the Republic of Korea as an open society— economically, militarily, culturally—are so dominant that they will not be overwhelmed by the north.

Economically, the south has overtaken the north by ten or fifteen years. Militarily, however, we are in a draw. What this means is that the south is now capable of defending itself by itself, as long as the north does not attack with outside help. One can derive no satisfaction however from victory in war.

The genuine victory comes only from subduing the enemy without a fight. This is why the south's military strength should continue to be increased until such time as our adversary is convinced that to start another war would be futile. Step by step, through our dedication to strengthen the nation's power on the basis of peace, *jaju* and democracy, we are marching steadily toward the vision of a unified Korea. Peace, *jaju* and democracy constitute processes as well as the results of our goal of unification. They are at once its means and an end.

Stability and Change in International Order

As we steadily pursue *jaju*, peace and democracy, we should exert special effort to make the international environment conducive to unification and to Korean advances into the world community. That the international environment in which we find ourselves today has become harder to master is an indication that it is in a period of important transition. Our country's security and development should be ensured by closely following international currents and exploring elements of stability in the midst of change.

For some time now, the world has been undergoing the slow process of transition from bipolarism to multipolarism. It was President Charles de Gaulle of France who, in the early 1960s, perceived that the Cold War was actually a monopolization of power between the Soviet Union and the United States. In search of the lost glory of France, he forged a path independent of these two powers.

From the latter part of 1960s, even the communist bloc, once considered monolithic, began to show clefts, with China and the Soviet Union beginning to quarrel. The process of the disintegration of traditional East-West bloc politics was furthered not only by the Big Powers' inability to wage nuclear war, but also by the emergence of such middle ranking powers as Japan, Europe and China. The active pursuit by Third World countries of their own interests, in the middle of this all, helped to complete the change. Today, the United States and the Soviet Union, although militarily still super powers, are no longer politically supreme.

Faced by the limits that an international order based on confrontation presents, the United States and the Soviet Union are exploring the path of détente, thus accelerating the development of a multipolar world. With the international order becoming so diversified, it has become the trend for more and more countries to pursue their own pragmatic courses over and above the limitations imposed by ideology.

Under the framework of the Cold War, with its clearly defined military and political alliances, many countries had little room to maneuver or make choices. In the state of complete confrontation involving the free world and communism, nation states that once played major roles in world history had to accept restricted spheres of action on the world stage. In almost all countries that were left divided by World War II, including of course Korea, ideology often took precedence over national interests. In the case of Korea, the Cold War requirement for maintaining the status quo seriously inhibited our aspiration for unification.

The simple logic of the Cold War no longer holds water in today's new international order. Whether in the East or West, ideological homogeneity has been so weakened that some even talk of the "death of ideology." Ideology is now being trimmed to meet the peculiar requirements of each country. Indeed, ideology alone has become irrelevant in international society; more and more weight is given to consideration of national requirements and interests. While not yet rejecting the essence of ideology, it is increasingly being considered right to trim or revise ideology to serve national interests and security. It is now a nation's ethos rather than universal ideology that is increasingly coming to the fore. This is how many nation states are emerging as chief actors on the world stage.

Despite efforts by the Big Powers to lessen tension

around the world, the change that has been recounted here has made it impossible for many countries to avoid an arms race, racial wars or disputes over natural resources. The result is perpetual tension, involving almost all countries.

Such a change in the structure of international society is bound to influence the Korean peninsula, which once bore the brunt of the Cold War. We took the initiative and proposed a south-north dialogue in an effort to help prevent the threat of war caused by changes in the international situation. But these continued changes offer us no room for optimism or wishful thinking. In the course of rapid transformation, freedom of choice certainly expands. But it should not be forgotten that with freedom comes increased risks and increased responsibility for results.

A multipolar world is certainly not a simple international environment. Unlike the Cold War days when dependence on the power of an ally was possible, we now have only ourselves to rely on, and at the same time we must carefully watch the moves of the United States, Japan, China, the Soviet Union and many other countries as well. This requires a high level of adaptability and creativeness.

The risks contained in the international situation of today are eloquently reflected in the trials and tribulations in which the world legal system finds itself. Having gone through two world wars and despite so many ideological conflicts, mankind has sought to peacefully solve disputes among nations within the framework of law and international organizations. The founding of the United Nations represented this effort. Although there is room for discussion on how effectively the United Nations has been able to contribute to the cause of international peace, most nations of the world have tried to confirm their existence in the community of nations through it, and whenever disputes have arisen among them, they have sought to peacefully resolve them through the world body. For many years, Korea, too, made the United Nations a major stage of diplomacy. It was the United Nations which supervised our first election, and when the north Korean invasion began, the United Nations came to our aid.

The United Nations' contributions in economic, social and cultural fields have been eye-opening, and its role in peacefully resolving a number of local wars cannot be ignored. Unfortunately, however, a considerable amount of skepticism exists about its effectiveness in the international community. As more and more member nations began to cast their ballots according to national interests, the symbol of the U.N. as the conscience of humanity and as the defender of the rule of law came under assault. With that trend, its capability to resolve important international security problems has also declined.

The weakening role of the United Nations is giving rise to the phenomenon of the so-called Big Power Politics. Certainly this is one of the most dangerous things for us to guard against. In the games that Big Powers play, it is not so simple to distinguish a friend from an enemy. Yesterday's friend can be abandoned without consideration, yesterday's adversary can be today's friend, and today's enemy can become tomorrow's negotiating partner. This is the nature and the reality of Big Power politics. Such virtues as loyalty, legalism or even human compassion are but *weaknesses* before the interlocking interests of the Big Powers; so is the old state of alliances which, depending on fluctuation of interests, could go through many metamorphoses according to relations of power. Accordingly, it is not hard to realize what a dangerous situation small countries are in. A living example of this sad state of affairs is Poland, whose territory has been dismembered many times in history. History records many more cases of countries that fell under colonialism because of Big Power politics.

Consider Korea's own recent history. Some of our forebears must of course share the blame for letting their country fall prey to Japan's colonial control. But it cannot be denied that the Big Powers at the time helped to bring this about. Some European powers, too preoccupied at the time with czarist Russia's eastward movement, concurred in allowing

Japan to seize the Korean Peninsula. Thus the international situation at the time worked adversely for Korea. With that piece of history in mind, we cannot let our vigilance down at the reemergence of Big Power politics. Just as an individual must protect himself, so a nation must consider security and survival as indispensable. When a nation's survival is at stake, politics, economy, culture, everything should be organized and mobilized for that single purpose.

Those who are capable of surviving and prospering within the Big Power political sphere are either Big Powers themselves or those countries which, although they are smaller, are capable of mobilizing a high degree of wisdom and capability to harmonize their relations with the Big Powers by quickly perceiving their intentions. Under such circumstances, Korea should wisely explore the path of independence by raising our vigilance against the subservience of consigning our destiny to an arrangement such as has been suggested, involving four or five Big Powers.

The international order today is complicated more than ever before by the question of the North-South crisis. The question revolves around a confrontation between the rich, industrial northern hemisphere and the poor, developing southern hemisphere. This confrontation, having already risen over the simple plane of economic inequity, has grown into a serious dispute threatening the peace and stability of the international community. With the gap between the two hemispheres widening instead of closing, the north-south confrontation is becoming ever more acute. Countries in the south, locked in the depth of poverty and hampered by shortages of capital as well as by worsening balances of payment, find themselves incapable of meeting the rising expectations of their people. Despair and frustration in the southern hemisphere is deepening.

Leaders of developing nations, blaming their poverty not on their traditional attitudes or ineptitude but on an unequal economic system inherited from colonial administrations, demand better trade terms and a restructuring of the international economic system. Most of these leaders even complain that economic aid from advanced nations, instead of growing as it allegedly should, is actually beginning to slacken.

Many richer nations of the world, confronted by the rising demands of their own people and the growing instability in the international economy, find it difficult to respond to these complaints. Moreover, with walls of protectionism being erected on goods coming from the developing world, the state of economic confrontation between the north and south is not likely to be solved very quickly. Although the Republic of Korea, thanks to its hard working people, is fast approaching the group of advanced countries, it is not in a position to sit with arms folded and ignore these complaints. Any renewed flareup of economic wars among nations could gravely affect the Korean economy, which must grow rapidly in spite of the heavier military burdens resulting from the planned departure of the American ground forces. The recent cartelization of the world's major raw materials, including oil, shows how fragile the world economy can be. In the event of another confrontation, and if the western countries retaliate with protectionism, the current international society will be thrown into uncontrollable chaos. These are some of the challenges and tribulations that the changing structure of international politics and economy now present to us. Nothing less than the total application of Korea's traditional wisdom and potential is required to cope with the risks that we must face before we can achieve national development and prosperity.

In examining the currents of the international situation and attempting to spotlight the reality behind them, Koreans learn that in security, diplomacy, economics and in almost every other field, they face the difficult challenge of having to seek dual goals—stability and change. Even in the evolving relations between south and north Korea, prevention of a renewed war may mean the need to stabilize the state of confrontation between the two sides and relations with the Big Powers. Creation of conditions for unification, however, requires changes in the situation surrounding Korea. The relation between defense and national security is not much different. While Korea's security must be ensured through the alliance with the United States and other major allies, the effort to create and strengthen a self-reliant defense must go on.

Looking back at the days of the Cold War, we find that the question of national security was much simpler and easier then. Among the nations within the free world, a broad relationship of credibility and fraternity existed. In time of emergency, friends could be counted upon. Not so any more. At a time when each nation is making its own calculations and seeking its own specific interests, we have only our own power to safeguard security and independence. Help is offered only when one helps oneself. When each country is concerned with its own interests, in the end, it is often the question of who is winning rather than who is right that decides the final outcome. In the case of Korea, our allies will begin to help us only after they are convinced that we, and not the north Korean Communists, are overwhelmingly superior.

The United States' decision to pull out its ground combat troops is posing a new challenge to the question of security but, come to think of it, we believe it can be turned into a chance to accelerate the process of establishing a self-reliant defense structure. Having long anticipated this course of development, the government had already made preparations for it by launching the Homeland Reserve Force and the Civil Defense Corps, designed to back up overall defense in time of war. The imposition of the defense tax and defense donations also contribute greatly to the modernization of the armed forces.

Not only materially but also in our mental preparedness, the south should be able to overcome the north and, for this purpose, we must strengthen total security. In war, our soldiers, from enlisted men to generals, are dedicated to victory. But a modern war is too complicated to be left to soldiers alone. Participation of people from all walks of life ensures the success of a modern war, which needs a total security system. It would be dangerous indeed to let our guard down at any slight improvement in the situation or a lull in the tension.

A national security system, even if 99 percent complete, is never perfect, for a 1 percent miscalculation could destroy the rest. A peaceful country like Switzerland, which has not fought a war for hundreds of years, enforces a strict, self-reliant defense policy by building antinuclear shelters and other facilities in preparation for an attack. Such a meticulous preparedness has spared Switzerland from foreign attack for two hundred years. During World War II, Nazi troops, in deference, skirted Switzerland in their march toward the conquest of other countries.

The wise adage that "a nation which loves war falls, but so does one that forgets," should be deeply ingrained in our mind. So long as the Communists in north Korea are capable of unleashing another war, Korea's defense should never be dependent on an ally. By strengthening material as well as psychological preparedness, peace must be maintained on the peninsula.

An independent diplomatic power is no less important than a self-reliant defense. A nation's strength is measured by its diplomatic skills as well as by its defense. We are aware of cases of countries which, though militarily weak, nevertheless succeed in maintaining their security through the power of diplomacy. Our capacity to shape a wise independent diplomacy is crucial in order for Korea to stabilize relations with the Big Powers and, from such relationships, to create a situation favorable to us. While Korea continues a policy of faith and fraternity with the free world in the midst of never ending changes in the international community, it should also act wisely on the matter of national security and prosperity to protect its interests in the world. On many occasions, the Republic of Korea has declared a policy of seeking exchanges and cooperation not only with Third World countries but also with members of the communist bloc and, with some of these countries, relations are on the way to improvement.

Particularly encouraging is the fact that, as Korea's strength increases, more and more nations around the world seek relations with us. Through cultural and economic relations with them and by skillfully combining goals with reality, Korea's position in the world is sure to become stronger. We are beginning to occupy a larger place in the world community, owing to our economic growth. This results in a stronger reaction to world recessions and stagnation, but at the same time, it means a larger contribution to stability. Korea's goal of rapidly reaching the level of advanced nations requires both material development and greater adaptability. As Korea's economy continues to grow, so will its contribution to the stability of the international economic order.

To recapitulate, seeking stability from change and change from stability constitutes the challenge and task faced by the Republic of Korea in the international community. To insure survival and protect security, the base of relations with allies will continue to be broadened. On the one hand, our independence must be strengthened; on the other, economic and diplomatic interests must be pursued and preserved. While swiftly reacting to changes in international developments, active efforts should not be spared to channel these changes to benefit our cause.

The influence that a nation exercises in international society depends on the extent of national power as well as how effectively it is utilized. So far, we have wisely reacted to changes in the international situation by strenuously promoting national strength; but from now on more wisdom will be required. Safeguarding national security, protecting national independence, combining goals with reality, maturing and making a contribution to world society—the promotion of all of these diversified goals requires strong national power and adaptability. Herein lies our challenge and our opportunity.

An Era of Active Contribution

Seldom are great peoples captives of their past glory or prisoners of their present advantages. Rather, they live in an awareness of a future mission and its realization. Insight into that mission is gained by projecting the past and present into the future. Its significance can be seen by relating it to the flow of world history.

In opening a new era of national regeneration, Korea will not find satisfaction in securing stability, prosperity and unification only for its own sake. Through accumulated strength and model behavior, we will find satisfaction as we seek to make a fitting contribution to the peace and prosperity of the world, as well.

Making a worthy contribution to the progress of world history should hardly be the prerogative of Big Powers. Japan, deprived of its military might, does so through economic power; a small ancient people like the Jews do so through their religious inspiration. The door is wide open for every country to make its fair contribution to international society. In the present transition from an old order to a new one, problems such as population, war, pollution, and a paucity of natural resources are rending the world apart. In every country, the traditional way of living and social system has been challenged by change and confusion. From the depth of such instability, more and more people are beginning to search for wisdom and knowledge to tide them over the crisis of civilization.

Perhaps our traditional concept of peace might offer a modest contribution to the cause of world peace and stability. The spirit of peace as manifested in the Saga of Beneficial Man or the nonviolent pacifism of the 1919 March First Independence Movement, appealing as it did to the principle of human justice and self-determination of people, are expressions of Korea's confidence to maintain harmonious relations among nations. These spirits are the basis of the attitude and ethics necessary to bring about a unified Korea or for all nations to live peacefully as a world family.

It is often forgotten that, although the world is torn apart by conflict and strife, it is fated to live in interdependence. Developments in communications and transportation have sharply reduced the size of the world, making it essential for nations to cooperate and carry on exchanges with each other. All forms of conflict, whether they involve racial differences, ideology or natural resources, have to be resolved through dialogue in a peaceful manner. I have long asserted that the nations of the world should fling their doors open; that to solve their mounting problems, it should remain our unchanging policy to promote mutual exchanges and cooperation.

Of particular concern today is the deepening trend of protectionism. Although it originated from the simple desire of each nation to protect itself from the shocks of world economic crisis, protectionism in effect not only deepens the crisis but even damages long-term interests. In the present day world, which is sustained by international trade and by an international division of labor, long-term harmony and cooperation should take precedence over short-term egoism or myopia. The common development of humankind is possible only through such a broad pattern of endeavor.

For a single nation or community of nations, the principle of common development through cooperation should be the same. Just as the *Saemaul* spirit effected the rehabilitation of villages and the development of the nation, so its spirit, when practiced among nations, should enable them to cross over the barriers of myopic national interests. The individual who is only concerned for his own well-being cannot contribute to the prosperity of the nation, and the nation which only seeks its own interest, simply adds to the confusion and danger of the world community.

The economic development that Korea has made so far, through the hard work of its people, enables it, I believe, to render a considerable contribution to the solution of global economic problems through wider exchanges and cooperation. With our status changing from an aid-receiving nation to a donor nation, Korea should be able to offer economic or technical aid to developing countries to help them rise from poverty. Korean aid will be based on quality rather than quantity and have more of a spiritual than of a material value. Its true role will be to emphasize the sharing of experiences with countries that are going through the phases that we have passed. The pattern of our economic development can be a source of hope and encouragement to many. But we must demonstrate the hard work involved in development rather than just the visible, showy results.

Our *Saemaul* spirits of diligence, self-help and cooperation might be useful for other developing countries now trying to awaken themselves. We claim a modest credit for Korea's present economic development. Our experimentation with democratic institutions and the spiritual revolution could serve as a model for developing countries seeking a similar way to modernization. The operation of our democratic system has been made even more efficient by the recovery of Korea's traditions of harmony, cooperation and creativeness. The *Saemaul* movement has made it possible for us to attain, without outside help, the ideals and aspirations of the Korean people.

By encouraging free enterprise and the freedom of businessmen, the government and business have achieved a more cooperative relationship. By successfully coping with the ills of materialism and the problems of alienation in society, Korea, overall, is being led on a more humane and compassionate course. These multiple factors of growth in Korea should certainly be presented as a recommendable way of development.

Each country's development reflects its own historical peculiarity. That being the case, there is no assurance, of course, that our way of solving problems could automatically be applied to others. If our model could one day cross over national borders and conceivably solve the problems of others, then we would have served our purpose.

Beginning with our closest neighbors, we will endeavor to share the spirit of peace and cooperation. Although geographically far removed from us, East-West civilizations at one time focused on the nations of Asia and the Pacific. Since the end of the World War II, some of these nations have become hot spots of the Cold War. For the Republic of Korea to try to seek political, economic, social and cultural relations with these nations is not only desirable but logical. In this age of multipolarism, it has become the general trend for neighboring nations to reinforce their cooperative ties. Especially in view of the growing importance that Asia and the Pacific have assumed, we can say that to seek peace, stability, and prosperity in this region will be to contribute to the development of the world community.

The achievement of peace and cooperation among nations, based on Korea's outstanding cultural values, would be a positive contribution to the shaping of a world culture. Although the international community today is said to form one cultural sphere, it cannot be denied that Western values have played a dominant role. For a genuine world culture to flourish, however, it must reflect within itself aspects of all other cultures and traditions. A world culture can claim to represent a true cosmopolitanism when it achieves harmony in diversity. When a world culture is shaped by the participation of peoples around the world, it will then have helped to create the peace and prosperity which have remained humanity's dream for a long time. A genuine peace among nations would then be supported by common ethics and morality that arise from a single culture.

With some nations still believing in the principle of the survival of the fittest, these hopes and ideals will hardly be realized soon. Some nations do not hesitate to flout international law or human conscience. Even though a part of today's international political reality is affected by these blind pursuits of egotism, they are but a temporary aberration when seen from the perspective of human civilization. Law, ethics, morality, equality, faith, credibility—these are still the main elementary ingredients which sustain relations among nations. Permanent peace and prosperity in the international community are possible through the rule of law over naked force and strife, through harmony and cooperation taking precedence over conflict.

While we will seek to cope wisely with the reality of uncertain power politics, we shall spare no efforts to anchor a peaceful world order by strengthening national power and by continuing to be friendly and faithful to allies. It is the lofty mission of the great Korean people to overcome the greatest tragedies of the twentieth century, poverty and war, and to achieve prosperity and peace. The fulfillment of this mission will bring us honor.

Conclusion:
Korea's Path to Regeneration

Conclusion

Seldom is national development or social transformation achieved without new challenges and problems. Nations that rise from tradition-bound societies to open new epochs of industrialization always meet these challenges boldly, and by successfully coping with them, give prominence to their collective wisdom. In short, development is a succession of problems and solutions.

By wiping out premodern elements from our tradition, Korea has almost miraculously modernized itself. Now, by rising to attack the problems modernization creates, Koreans are about to open a new chapter in their history—the regeneration of their nation. The ills and pains caused by modernization efforts must be controlled by our own determination. By reawakening the strength of our long traditions, the nation must move speedily to bigger developments. The path we choose to take is a virgin path taken by none before. It is an opportunity to write our names on a chapter of world history.

What other people in the world share the same military threat that confronts us? Which aggressive force could match the hostility and adventurism of north Korea's? How many countries are there in the world which are as vulnerable as we are to even the slightest stirrings by the world powers that crowd our borders? These, then, are adversities against which we must preserve our survival and security.

What Korea needs today is stronger national power.

We must write a new chapter in history about Korea's regeneration by steadily improving national power. It is our generation's lofty mission, worthy of fulfillment. When this mission is successfully accomplished, future historians will proudly note how the Korean people, by rising to the challenges of a hostile international environment, have created stability, prosperity and peace for themselves.

The path that we take, history will record, leads to our nation's goals. Korea, through its arduous economic construction, has rediscovered its hidden potential. The Korean people have become convinced that they, too, can now have affluence. The Korean people are on their way to rediscovering their forefathers' wisdom and spirit, which have been preserved over five thousand years. What we see is a picture of a heroic people who have survived many foreign invasions, many forms of adversity. It is a picture of creative and cultural people who have created original things by blending foreign cultures with their own, even while undergoing never-ending problems.

We are also on the way to rediscovering, bit by bit, the ancient spirits of *jaju*, harmony and creativeness growing out of a history of thousands of years. It is not past glory we seek, but wisdom for the future. It is not a simple national idiosyncracy we seek, but Korea's unique spiritual character worthy of enriching world culture. By seeking to blend Western civilization with the spiritual values of the East, we also seek a new national identity for ourselves. By reviving the ancient wisdom of our forefathers, we seek a spiritual revolution and the growth of man. It is a highly developed form of civilization that we pursue, without the usual spiritual emptiness. On our way to an organized, mass industrial society, we propose to eliminate the side effect of dehumanization. We seek a civilization in which man, and not materialism, leads the spirit. Having ridden ourselves of the shackles of poverty and stagnation inherited from a tradition-bound society, having risen above the conflict and alienation growing out of modern society, Korea is on its way to building a society of harmony, cooperation and compassion.

We have found the way to achieve these goals through the *Yushin* Reforms and *Saemaul* movement. By practicing the principles inherent in them, Korea has finally controlled poverty. Our people's confidence and pride have been restored by the economic construction the nation has achieved. The *Yushin* Reforms have helped us to rediscover Korea's national identity; new life is being sought in ancient traditions, and many premodern aberrations are being corrected. Such is the process of building an orderly, stable, democratic society.

The path we choose to take leads to democracy. Korea's political democracy, as it is geared to preserving national survival and security, is nationalistic. It is democratic in the sense that its institutions have been freely chosen by the people. Korea's democratic system reflects the people's resolve to protect themselves from the threat of communism. It also reflects their ardent desire to attain prosperity and freedom.

Our political democracy is not a mishmash of political compromise that can be traded like articles in the market; it is a purposeful and creative endeavor, a productive political system requiring harmonious and cooperative spirits. Through a wider public participation, it becomes an effective instrument for giving form to the nation's aspirations, while helping to shape the foundation of total unity.

The *Saemaul* movement provides a training ground for productive education in political democracy by encouraging constructive dialogue and debate instead of petty political squabblings over unfamiliar issues. It is democracy in everyday life. Participation in *Saemaul* can be pleasant, as it involves neighbors; participation in *Saemaul* is also meaningful, because it attacks practical problems. The followers of the *Saemaul* movement, unlike members of a mass society, seldom give way to indifference or lethargy. Unlike the familiar picture of citizens of newly emerging nations, they seldom allow political passion to overtake them. *Saemaul* people are your next-door neighbors, who are interested in solving problems, and by doing so, are determined, in their own quiet way, to render a worthy service to the nation.

The path we choose to take leads to prosperity. We have shaped a society of affluence that our forefathers never achieved. By proudly joining the ranks of nations developing heavy and petrochemical industries, our generation has destroyed the myth that Korea was destined to perpetual poverty. The Korean economy's power to better react to international competitiveness has been strengthened by a sophisticated industrial structure and technological innovations. In quantitative and qualitative terms, the Korean economy is gradually resembling that of advanced nations; the gap between city and farm, between regions and classes is gradually diminishing. A better balance has been achieved in growth and development. An affluence has been created together, to be enjoyed together. Such affluence should provide all of us a fair share of food, shelter and clothing, a better education and health for all.

The path of prosperity we choose leads to peace. Through the power of liberty and prosperity, Korea is in pursuit of the national goal of peaceful unification. What use would unification have, if it were to rest on the ruins of war? While guarding against unification based on communism, which is being secretly plotted by the north Korean regime, or unification based on sentimentalism, Korea is seeking the consistent goal of unification based on peace, *jaju* and democracy.

The first step toward unification starts with the restoration of credibility through peaceful dialogue and exchange, so that peace can be firmly anchored on the peninsula. It is not a negative peace, punctuated by periodic tension, that we see; it is rather a positive peace capable of bringing the two sides into cooperation in mutual confidence. We follow the road to peace that preceding generations explored for five thousand years, the road that links Korea with the rest of the world.

It is through *jaju* and Korea's proud cultural traditions that we desire to contribute to world peace and prosperity. Korea's security should be ensured through an equitable balancing of the Big Powers; common interests pursued through the harmonizing of the desires of all nations; dialogue and cooperation expanded on the basis of *jaju* to improve relations with Korea's allies. Peace should not mean a dependence, but interdependence; it should not mean isolation, but an open society based on *jaju*.

How many times throughout the five thousand years of our history has any generation been presented with greater challenges than these? Indeed, they are challenges to our ability, a chance for our generation to write a new chapter in history. There is a strong impact from this transformation. We feel the pain of shedding our old skin; we feel the birth-pain of a brighter future. Had the previous generation successfully endured such pains a hundred years ago, they would have handed us a different historical condition. We have drawn a painful lesson from their failure, by adding a new chapter of the regeneration of Korea. Having successfully pulled through so many tribulations and so much hardship, the Korean people now open their gate to usher in a shining civilization formed by their never-dying potential.

Our generation's goal is clear; our path definite. Who shall, in the face of this lofty mission, allow himself to fall behind others in the march toward its accomplishment? Who could dare turn his back on its lofty value? The path to Korea's national regeneration is the path over which all Koreans must march; it is the act of creating a new history together. In this phase of creation, we—all of us—are present to play our role.

Index

Index

advanced industrialized society, 108
affluent society, 12, 16, 94, 97, 104, 110, 145
agricultural development, 73-74
alienation, 137, 144
American presidential system, 39
antistate activities, 44

basic rights of citizens, 44, 51
Big Power guarantee for Korea's unification, 123
Big Power politics, 129-30
bipolarism, 126
bipolar structure of the world, 114
British parliamentary government, 39
Buddhism-for-National-Salvation, movement 22, 27

Chusok (Korean Thanksgiving Day), 124
Civil Defense Corps, 132
civil liberties, 51
class struggle, 118
Closed Door Policy, 31
closed economic system, 93
Cold War, 48, 56, 114, 117, 126-28, 132, 138

Communism, 94, 118, 122, 125, 127, 144-45
Communist Bloc, 56, 126, 134
community center, 81
compassionate society, 105
Confucianism, 28, 30

death of ideology, 127
defense donations, 132
defense tax, 132
de Gaulle constitution, 45
dehumanization, 34, 105, 143
Demilitarized Zone, 49
democracy, 27, 38-39, 41-47, 51, 57-60, 80-81, 122, 126, 144-45
democracy's principle of compromise, 41
democratic government, 39
democratic institutions, 59, 137
democratic leadership, 82
democratic political system, 38, 40
democratic social development, 81
democratic society, 16, 51-52, 59, 64-65, 80-81, 144
democratic unification, 121-22
destructive minority, 52
détente, 127
developing country, 7, 42, 97, 137
direct democracy, 80

distribution of wealth, 102
division of power, 54

East-West bloc politics, 126
East-West détente, 49
economic development, 7, 41-42,
    63, 71, 83, 91, 96-97,
    102-3, 136-37
economic self-reliance, 12, 71, 92
80,000 Woodblock Prints, 30
emergency powers, 44
environmental improvement pro-
    jects, 74
environmental protection cam-
    paign, 103-4
equality, 27, 29, 47, 51-52, 139
export-led industrialization, 73
external-oriented development
    strategy, 72

Factory *Saemaul* Movement, 102-3
Five-Year Economic Development
    Plans, 70-72, 90, 92
Foreign Policy for Peace and Unifi-
    cation, 56
freedom, 29, 51-52, 57, 119, 128,
    144
free economy, 93, 99
free enterprise system, 101, 137
free society, 86, 94
free world, 127, 133

garrison society, 125
genuine political democracy, 47
global community, 115
gross national product, 95

Hangul (the Korean alphabet), 15,
    29
heterogeneity between the south
    and north, 124

high economic growth with stabil-
    ity, 98, 100, 104
high economic growth policy, 73,
    96, 99
highly industrialized society,
    94-95, 105, 114
Homeland Reserve Force, 132
human dignity, 51, 108
Hwabaek System, 30
Hwankok, 30
Hwarang Knights, 22, 27

identity, 19-20, 35, 38, 122
ideological homogeneity, 127
income gaps, 102
independent diplomacy, 133
individualism, 26, 60, 65, 83
industrial ethics of modern time, 76
international communism, 117, 125
international community, 17, 129-
    30, 133-34, 138-39
international power politics, 48
International Youth Skill Olympics,
    93

jaju (political independence), 12,
    21-24, 29-30, 33, 35, 48,
    57, 62, 78, 83, 86-87, 97,
    102, 104, 108, 116, 118,
    121-22, 126, 143, 145-46
Japan's colonial rule, 13, 33, 129
July Fourth South-North Joint
    Communique, 56, 123

Kingdom of *Koguryo,* 15, 22, 27
Kingdom of *Koryo,* 22, 30
Kingdom of *Paekche,* 15, 27
Kingdom of *Silla,* 15, 22, 27, 30,
    119

King *Sejong,* 15, 31, 85
Korean Empire, 48
Korean peninsula, 15, 48-49, 114,
    120, 122, 128, 130
Korean War, 50, 71, 117, 121, 123
Korea's liberation from Japan, 59,
    64, 93, 116-17
kye (mutual assistance societies), 77

labor-management relationship,
    103
legalism, 65
Leninism, 118
lesson of Indochina, 55
life ethics, 26, 57

Mandate of Heaven, 27, 32
March First Independence Move-
    ment, 24, 121, 135
Marxism, 118
mass consumer society, 61
mass society, 60, 105, 144
materialism, 83, 105, 137, 143
members of the divided families,
    119
Miracle by the Han River, 91
modern bourgeois society, 80
modern democratic institutions, 47
modern industrial nation, 47
modernization, 7, 13, 16, 24,
    29-30, 33-34, 42-43, 47,
    51, 55, 63, 70, 73, 75, 86,
    101, 105, 137, 142
modernization movement, 20, 35,
    70
modernization of the armed forces,
    132
modernization strategy, 94
Mongols, 22, 30
multipolarism, 126, 138

nation state, 127
National Assembly, 53
national awareness, 3
National Conference for Unifica-
    tion, 52, 53
national consensus, 53, 55, 80, 125
national development, 77-78, 86,
    94, 131, 136, 142
national identity, 21, 32, 143-44
national independence, 16, 23, 134
national interest, 127, 129, 136
nationalist movement, 85
national legitimacy, 16, 117-18, 122
national regeneration, 15, 21, 38,
    57, 63, 82-83, 85, 95,
    115, 135, 141-42, 146
national salvation, 21, 23, 62
national security, 47, 51, 86, 127,
    132-34, 144
national spirit, 118, 122-24
national unification, 15, 115
nation building, 7, 67
nation's ethos, 127
neighborhood democracy, 80
new democratic ethic, 88
new industrial state, 89
nihilism, 106
Nixon Doctrine, 48
north Korean Communists, 117,
    122-23, 132-33
north Korean Communist regime,
    43, 49, 51, 56, 94, 96,
    117-19, 124, 145
North-South crisis, 130
Northeast Asia, 48, 115, 120
notion of *Ch'unghyo,* 28, 29
nuclear war, 129

oil crisis of 1973, 92
one-party dictatorship, 42
open society, 46, 56, 63, 86, 93,
    125, 146

patriotism, 28, 57, 62, 80, 87
peaceful unification, 53, 56, 68,
    95, 121, 145
Philosophy of Beneficial Man, 26,
    135
political democracy, 39, 68, 80,
    144
political democratization, 16
political development, 37, 59
political liberalization, 125
political stability, 38, 43, 45, 47,
    94, 114
politics of imitation, 40
pollution, 104, 135
power politics, 139
pragmatism, 33
principle of autonomy, 80
principle of diligence, self-help,
    and cooperation, 68
productive democracy, 58-59, 63
productive democratic system, 47,
    50, 56-57, 82
productive majority, 61
productive politics, 55, 65
protectionism, 97, 131, 136
Protestant Ethic, 32
pseudo-cosmopolitanism, 87
Puritans, 33
p'umatsi (working in turn for one
    another), 77

rationalism, 33, 40-41, 60
Reconstruction Movement, 75
recovery of humanism, 108
Reformation, 33
Renaissance Movement, 108
Republic of Korea, 38, 40, 43,
    46-47, 51-53, 55-56,
    90-91, 94, 121, 125, 131,
    133-34, 138
responsible democratic citizen, 81

rule of law, 40-41, 65, 129, 139
rule of virtue, 65

Saemaul education, 84
Saemaul leader, 81-82, 84
Saemaul (New Community) move-
    ment, 7, 16, 63, 67-70,
    75-83, 88, 102-3, 109-10,
    137, 144
Saemaul spirit, 73, 80, 84, 110,
    136-37
Saemaul village, 109
Saemaum (New Spirit) movement,
    83, 88, 110
self-identity, 20, 108, 119
self-reliant defense, 96, 132-33
self-sufficiency in rice, 69, 90
sense of collective destiny, 62
Silhak School, 30
simultaneous entry into the United
    Nations, 124
Sino-U.S. détente, 49
social development, 29, 38, 40-42,
    63, 88
social justice, 52
social welfare programs, 52
South-North dialogue, 50, 56, 120,
    125, 128
South-North nonaggression agree-
    ment, 120, 123-25
spirit of harmony and cooperation,
    63, 65
spirit of nonviolent pacifism, 121
spiritual revolution, 50, 73, 83-84,
    87-88, 137, 143
strategic industries, 99
strategy of internationalization, 97

Tang, kingdom of China, 22
Third World countries, 56, 121,
    126-27, 133

38th Parallel, 117
Three Principles of Peaceful Unification, 120
totalitarianism, 44
total security system, 132-33
trusteeship for Korea, 117
Turtle Ships, 30

Uich'ang, 30
underground tunnels for clandestine aggression, 123
Unification of the Three Kingdoms, 31
unified Korea, 50, 94, 120, 123, 126, 135
United Nations, 117, 128-29
United Nations Supervisory Commission, 117
urbanization, 29, 73, 83, 108

value system, 34, 64, 77, 106, 108
village parliament, 81

War of *Imjin* (Hideyoshi Invasion), 22, 30
welfare state, 68
Western civilization, 34, 143
Western democracy, 39, 40, 44-45, 59, 60
Western political system, 40-41
Western rationalism, 65
withdrawal of U.S. ground forces from Korea, 48, 57, 96, 131-32
work ethics, 77-78
World War II, 42, 119, 127, 133, 138

Yi Dynasty, 15, 22-23, 30-31, 85
Yushin (Revitalizing) Reforms, 14, 16, 37, 47, 50-51, 55, 82-83, 144